OWN

YOUR PIECE OF THE EARTH

Everything You Need to Know about Mortgages
in Canada's Major Housing Markets

IRENE STRONG

For my kids

Though much of the mortgage content from these pages may not apply when you are ready to buy, the underlying theme will always be true.

Own your piece of this earth and do it as soon as you can. It will be worth it, I promise.

TABLE OF CONTENTS

LIFE STORY

MORTGAGES

INTRODUCTION

Mortgages can be scary. I'm a mortgage broker and even my heart races when it's time to apply for a new mortgage for my family.

My experience with my clients has also taught me that buying a home or completing a refinancing is often prompted by major life events, such as moving in with a partner, getting married, having a baby, accepting a new job, retiring, managing an unexpected career change, or losing a loved one.

Add the complexities of mortgage financing at these times, and it can feel almost insurmountable.

I get it. I've been there many times. I want to you to know there are ways to manage the stresses that come with financing your home. With the right resources, advice and planning, it's possible to eliminate it almost entirely—and to prepare for and manage the experience successfully.

Knowing its importance, I wanted to take a deeper look at how stress impacts us. In my research, I was particularly intrigued by the Holmes and Rahe Stress Scale.

2

In 1967, psychiatrists Thomas Holmes and Richard Rahe developed the exercise as part of their research assessing the health impact of stress. Participants are given a total "stress score" by adding the "life event units" experienced in the previous year. The higher the score, the research indicates, the higher the risk of future illness.

THE HOLMES AND RAHE STRESS SCORE

Score 11-150: Low to moderate risk of becoming ill in the near future
Score 150-299: Moderate to high risk of becoming ill in the near future
Score 300-600: High to very high risk of becoming ill in the near future

LIFE EVENT	UNITS
Death of a spouse	100
Divorce	73
Marital separation	65
Imprisonment	63
Death of a close family member	63
Personal injury or illness	53
Marriage	50
Dismissal from work	47
Marital reconciliation	45
Retirement	45
Change in health of family member	44
Pregnancy	40
Sexual difficulties	39
Gain a new family member	39
Business readjustment	39

LIFE EVENT	UNITS
Change in financial state	38
Change in frequency of arguments	35
Major mortgage	32
Foreclosure of mortgage or loan	30
Change in responsibilities at work	29
Child leaving home	29
Trouble with in-laws	29
Outstanding personal achievement	28
Spouse starts or stops work	26
Begin or end school	26
Change in living conditions	25
Revision of personal habits	24
Trouble with boss	23
Change in working hours or conditions	20
Change in residence	20
Change in schools	20
Change in recreation	19
Change in church activities	19
Change in social activities	18
Minor mortgage or loan	17
Change in sleeping habits	16
Change in number of family reunions	15
Change in eating habits	15
Vacation	13
Christmas	12
Minor violation of law	11

I did the calculations for some hypothetical scenarios that include the life events that tend to trigger the need for a mortgage or a refinance.

I also added real life to the mix. For example, in the year you have a baby, you're also likely to experience a change in work hours or conditions (20 units), as well as changes in sleeping habits (16 units), social activities (18 units) and eating habits (15 units). There may be more arguments (24 units), time spent with extended family (15 units), holiday celebrations (12 units) and financial pressures (38 units).

The results of these hypothetical scenarios are head-spinning. The stress levels of people applying for a mortgage or a refinance in the same year they go through a divorce or have a baby topped the charts, with 452 and 535 units, respectively. Only one homeowner, the retiree, was under the 300-unit, highest-risk threshold in the year they made changes to their mortgage.

Other scenarios not addressed, such as planning home renovations, starting a business or going back to school, could also add up to extremely high stress scores.

In the chart outlining these scenarios, I have left a space for you (and your partner, if you have one) to do your own assessment of your past year and see how your stress score compares.

If you prefer to complete an online chart that tallies your score for you, *google: MindTools The Holmes and Rahe Stress Scale.*

HYPOTHETICAL LIFE EVENT SCENARIOS
MORTGAGE BUYERS AND REFINANCERS

LIFE EVENT	LIFE EVENT UNITS	GETTING MARRIED	HAVING A BABY	ILLNESS TO FAMILY MEMBER	DIVORCE	RETIREMENT	LOSS OF JOB	DEATH OF A SPOUSE	YOU	YOUR PARTNER
Death of a spouse	100	0	0	0	0	0	0	100		
Divorce	73	0	0	0	73	0	0	0		
Marital separation	65	0	0	0	0	0	0	0		
Imprisonment	63	0	0	0	0	0	0	0		
Death of a close family member	63	0	0	0	0	0	0	0		

LIFE EVENT	LIFE EVENT UNITS	GETTING MARRIED	HAVING A BABY	ILLNESS TO FAMILY MEMBER	DIVORCE	RETIREMENT	LOSS OF JOB	DEATH OF A SPOUSE	YOU	YOUR PARTNER
Personal injury or illness	53	0	0	53	0	0	0	0		
Marriage	50	50	0	0	0	0	0	0		
Dismissal from work	47	0	0	0	0	0	47	0		
Marital reconciliation	45	0	0	0	0	0	0	0		
Retirement	45	0	0	0	0	45	0	0		
Change in health of family member	44	0	44	44	0	0	0	44		
Pregnancy	40	0	40	0	0	0	0	0		
Sexual difficulties	39	0	39	0	0	0	0	0		
Gain a new family member	39	39	39	0	0	0	0	0		
Business readjusment	39	0	0	0	0	0	0	0		
Change in financial state	38	38	38	38	38	38	38	38		
Change in frequency of arguments	35	0	35	0	35	0	0	0		
Major mortgage	32	32	32	32	32	0	0	32		
Foreclosure of mortgage or loan	30	0	0	30	0	0	30	0		
Change in responsibilities at work	29	0	29	29	0	29	29	29		
Child leaving home	29	0	0	0	29	0	0	0		
Trouble with in-laws	29	29	29	0	29	0	0	0		
Outstanding personal achievement	28	0	0	0	0	0	0	0		
Spouse starts or stops work	26	0	26	26	0	0	26	0		

LIFE EVENT	LIFE EVENT UNITS	GETTING MARRIED	HAVING A BABY	ILLNESS TO FAMILY MEMBER	DIVORCE	RETIREMENT	LOSS OF JOB	DEATH OF A SPOUSE	YOU	YOUR PARTNER
Begin or end school	26	0	0	0	0	0	0	0		
Change in living conditions	25	25	25	25	25	25	0	25		
Revision of personal habits	24	24	24	24	24	24	24	24		
Trouble with boss	23	0	0	0	0	0	23	0		
Change in working hours or conditions	20	0	20	20	0	20	20	20		
Change in residence	20	20	20	0	20	20	0	0		
Change in schools	20	0	0	0	20	0	0	0		
Change in recreation	19	19	19	0	19	19	0	0		
Change in church activities	19	19	0	0	19	0	0	0		
Change in social activities	18	18	18	18	18	18	18	18		
Minor mortgage or loan	17	0	0	0	0	17	17	0		
Change in sleeping habits	16	16	16	16	16	16	16	16		
Change in number of family reunions	15	15	15	15	15	0	0	15		
Change in eating habits	15	15	15	15	15	0	15	15		
Vacation	13	13	0	0	13	13	0	0		
Christmas	12	12	12	12	12	0	12	12		
Minor violation of law	11	0	0	0	0	0	0	0		
TOTAL		384	535	397	452	284	315	388		

6

My point is not to say, "Do not buy property or get a mortgage—it's way too stressful, and you're likely to get sick." That's not at all what I want to stress. As you will learn in this book, mortgages are a powerful investment tool that can help you grow your wealth and ultimately achieve greater freedom and peace of mind.

· By recognizing that stress will be associated with these important and challenging life events, you can prepare for it.

One of the best ways to prepare is to learn. Arm yourself with an understanding of what to expect and why. By getting the information and expert advice you need, you can minimize uncertainty and make the best possible decisions for you and your family.

This book is designed with that in mind, to help you avoid unfortunate surprises and focus your energy and attention on the essential factors that will help you be prepared, save some money and understand what's important—to protect yourself and those you love.

As a mortgage professional, my job is to make sure my clients understand their mortgage options, feel comfortable with the mortgage product chosen and know *why* it's their best option in terms of meeting their overall objectives.

And if life changes, as life does, I am always available to help make sure their mortgage continues to align with their needs and dreams. I'm proud to be part of a profession that shares these values.

This book is an extension of my commitment to continuously expand my ability to help my clients leverage their mortgage to achieve their financial and life goals—with the least possible amount of stress. And, of course, the least amount of cost.

The next 200 or so pages are about mortgages and how they can be used to your advantage, but it's also a story about life because the two are never separate. While I'm trained as a mortgage broker, I also have on-the-ground experience gained while pursuing my dream: growing a small real estate empire in one of Canada's hottest, most highly valued markets.

By sharing the story of how I (and then my husband and I) made decisions and managed risks while investing in real estate, my aim is to equip you with a basic understanding of mortgages and home buying. I want you to have the comfort that comes from knowing you are in control—and that you're not alone. You'll also find exercises designed to help you map your own, unique-to-you path.

8   We will dive into the more technical aspects of mortgages and how they work. All this information may look a bit daunting initially, but I guarantee it will save you time—and could save you tens or even hundreds of thousands of dollars in unnecessary interest over the long term. Many of my clients first came to me after spending many hours surfing the internet, not knowing they didn't even know what questions to google or ask.

This book was written for them, and for you.

CHAPTER 1
What *Is* a Mortgage?

A mortgage is one of the most powerful wealth-building tools available. This book provides the information and insights you need to use that tool—effectively and proactively—to realize your dreams.

While your mortgage will always appear in the liabilities column of your net worth statement, it is a debt that forces you to save and build **equity**. It can also make it possible to access investment opportunities far beyond simply owning your home.

Understanding the words, concepts and processes governing mortgages can, therefore, have a huge impact on your future wealth.

From a lender's perspective, a mortgage is an investment secured by your property. It's also a legal contract. The lender's return on investment (ROI) is the interest you agree to pay. In the mortgage contract, therefore, there is almost always a clause that states that you'll have to pay a penalty if you pay back the loan before the **maturity date**. (Much more on that later.)

12 Further, if you stop making payments during the mortgage term, the lender will proceed with legal action, called **foreclosure**, to get the money they loaned you back by selling the property.

No lender wants to go through the foreclosure proceedings. It's a long and costly process that puts their investment at risk. That's why there is a great deal of emphasis placed on the upfront review and qualification of mortgage applicants, to avoid ever having to foreclose. We call this underwriting: the process of ensuring borrowers have the capacity to make their mortgage payments through to the end of the term.

Canadians typically do not default on their mortgages. Our arrears rates in the second quarter of 2017 fell to the lowest levels in decades, a quarter of a percent (0.25%). Strong lending guidelines and underwriting by our financial institutions, along with a cultural tendency to pay on time, means that most Canadians (including you), will not default.

LINGO!

EQUITY
The portion of the value of a home belonging to a homeowner after the mortgage and any other debts owed on the property are subtracted. As the principal on the mortgage loan is paid, the equity usually increases. Increases in market value and improvements made to the home may add to equity as well.

MATURITY DATE
The day the mortgage contract ends. The mortgage can be paid in full, refinanced, renewed or switched to a new lender without penalty on this day.

FORECLOSURE

If a borrower defaults on a loan—that is, stops making payments as agreed in the mortgage contract—a lender will proceed with legal action to get the court's permission to take possession of the property and sell it to recover the unpaid debt.

13

From a broker's perspective, my perspective, there are a few times in life where taking a bit of extra time to learn some basic concepts can make a significant difference in your financial future. This is one of them.

Most industries have their own language, abbreviations and acronyms, and the mortgage industry is no different. "Lingo" makes life easier, simpler and more efficient for those within the industry, but it can mean that something may be lost in translation for the very person who needs to understand it most.

For example, I went to physio for my knee and was learning hard, awkward new exercises. In one session, the physiotherapist was explaining a new stretch. As I did my best to follow her directions, she said, "That's good, but you need to dorsiflex your foot more."

It caught me off guard. Never did I think I would hear that word again. Fortunately, I studied kinesiology in university and was familiar with the term dorsiflexion. For those who are curious, I have provided an illustration, since I believe it's the easiest way to explain it.

The take-a-way is: how many physio clients have a degree in kinesiology? Unfamiliar language can make even simple actions such as dorsiflexion and plantarflexion extremely confusing.

When it comes to mortgages, I want to help you turn "dorsiflexion" into "point your toes to the sky."

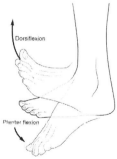

CREDIT | Dorsi and plantar flexion of the foot. Photo by Connexions - http://cnx.org, CC BY 3.0, https://commons.wikimedia.org/w/index.php?curid=29624326

I want things to make sense, so you are confident making decisions. I also want you to feel comfortable with mortgage lingo. When clients and experts speak the same language, it provides a kind of shorthand that speeds our work together and can make it more effective, positive and long-lasting.

I urge you to call a timeout and ask questions of your mortgage broker *whenever* you don't feel entirely clear on something. Knowing what things mean can help ensure you get the best mortgage for you, make the process as stress-free as possible and maximize the financial and emotional returns on your home.

I know mortgage lingo can be clear as mud, so anytime you see a word within a sentence in bold text, it means you can find a definition lower on the page or the following page, as you may have noticed earlier in this chapter. You may also find my thoughts on the term and its importance to you, in italics.

These terms are also included in the glossary, a final section dedicated to common concepts and terms within the mortgage industry. I encourage you to read the glossary and then use it as a reference point and refresher as you go through your own mortgage process. Finally, there is also an index to help you find important information quickly and easily.

Before we dig deep into the mortgage world, though, let's get to know each other a little bit. It is my hope that my experiences will inspire you on your own path to a home you love - and greater wealth.

CHAPTER 2
This Is Us

Main Characters

Irene Strong, me, your narrator:
High heels and running shoes; equally comfortable in the business world and many social circles. Fiery. Determined. A big-city girl born in a small town.

Mark Strong, my husband:
Glasses. Somewhat geeky. Equally loud at chewing and clapping. Growing bald spot. An all-around nice guy who achieved everything he set out to do (as documented in his high school yearbook bio) before his 10-year reunion. A golf pro, he loves to regularly remind his wife she married a professional athlete.

While driving to sign the papers for our fourth property purchase together—the third property Mark hadn't seen before we bought it—I asked him to describe himself to me.

He looked confused, so I explained that I was looking for the kind of descriptions that introduce characters in screenplays. I gave him an example:

Bill Jones, 30, dancer. Never meant to be a dad; it just happened. He's been other things: postal worker, cab driver, bouncer, store clerk—never meant to be them either. Now he runs a daddy day care.

Mark, wanting to play a little, said we should "do each other" for fun. He started describing me, cleverly echoing the short, to-the-point phrases.

"How'd I do?" he asked when he finished. I could tell he was proud of his work.

Now it was my turn to do him, but I didn't know where to begin. I tapped the keyboard of my laptop, making a nervous clicking noise.

Finally, he started: "Glasses." I added, "Somewhat geeky." He kept going, addressing what he believes are his more annoying qualities. He smiled at the end. "Until only recently, didn't realise his talents as a writer."

So that's us. Sort of.

We're a pretty stereotypical middle-class Canadian family. We both attended university, started our careers and married before the age of 30. We own a home and two cars. We have two kids, a boy and a girl. We live in suburbia in BC's lower mainland—three bridges from downtown Vancouver in a neighbour-hood of detached houses now valued at about a million dollars apiece, the new norm for the region. The only thing missing is the family dog. (Allergies. Sigh.) We consider ourselves fortunate and are so grateful for the family and friends who helped us along the way, encouraging us as we pushed ourselves to achieve our goals.

As with most people, our story starts at the beginning, with the way we grew up.

My parents didn't have much money back then, but they managed to make the most of what they had, making a conscious decision to own property even when it was a stretch. To make it work, they became extremely resourceful.

I grew up with three older siblings on an acreage where my dad established his first piano museum, which we occasionally referred to as a "piano farm."

19

When I was eight, we moved to Revelstoke, BC. My parents converted a Victorian home, a community historical landmark, into a piano museum and bed and breakfast, The Piano Keep. Most of my childhood was spent surrounded by pianos. Likely around a hundred—we never counted. Having pianos, and lots of them, was normal to us. You might think we were well off. We weren't, but my parents' remarkable passion, love and savvy made it possible for us to survive and thrive.

In this and so many other ways, I know my upbringing was not "normal." I'm so grateful—it made me who I am today and will continue to define me in the years to come.

Mark's family moved many times during his childhood as his dad was promoted in his career with BC credit unions. With each new job, they sold their home and bought another in the new town, typically near the local golf course where Mark's dad could practice his preferred pastime. His mom worked in banking, and then later as a part-time daycare provider while raising the kids.

Mark and I met in Revelstoke. We were friends, best friends. That was all. Fast forward to 2007, in Vancouver—we'd finally found a time to reconnect, 10 years after the first time we met. This time, something was different.

Now you.

Main Characters

Your Name

Your character sketch, or "elevator pitch"—how would you describe yourself to a potential new best friend?

Do you have a partner? If so, ask him or her for a description or switch places and describe each other.

If you don't have a partner, but would like one at some point in the future, consider using this as an opportunity to list the 10 deal-breaker qualities you're looking for. Why? Because it's fun to think about—and because you'll never find Mr. or Ms. Right until you have a search image, so why not start getting clear on the details right now?

Your Partner's Name

Now, take a few minutes to write down the things you've learned in your life so far that help equip you for building your own real estate plan, whether you envision a house with a white-picket fence, cabin on the lake, or a multibillion-dollar rental property portfolio. Include both positive and negative lessons you've learned by watching the people around you. Did your mom teach you to live well while being thrifty about the things that didn't matter? Did you know someone who worried about money to the point it wasn't possible to enjoy life, something you want to avoid? Did you have a family member who always seemed ready to take a calculated risk to make life better? Reviewing these early lessons can help you understand where your financial tendencies, habits and perspectives come from—and to leave behind the ones that aren't serving you well.

CHAPTER 3
Oxford Street

In most ways, I am just a regular Joe (Irene) doing regular things, like pretty much everyone else. But I've noticed that I may be more likely than a lot of people to leap when I see opportunity.

Exhibit A: It is 2006, and while I don't know what I'm doing, I do know owning a home means more to me than owning a car. Work is either a 12-minute bus ride or a 20-minute walk, and the bus is less reliable than my feet, so I usually walk. If a bus comes along when I'm near a stop, I hop on. If not, I'm at work in 20 minutes anyway.

I could afford a mortgage payment, but not a mortgage payment and a car payment, so I got rid of my car and bought a condo. It was a bit like my route to work—I walked rather than waiting for the bus because I wanted to always keep moving forward. That's what my first condo purchase represented to me. Moving forward.

I had just moved back to Vancouver for the second time in less than four months, this time to work in what I believed was my dream job. Growing up, I always wanted to be a professional athlete, specifically, an Olympic athlete. After realizing I was more likely to be struck by lightning than make Canada's team, I thought, "Hey, maybe I can work in the Olympics one day."

I went to university and graduated with a joint degree in management and kinesiology and aspirations of one day becoming a sports agent. Maybe for an Olympian?

I thought my dream of working in the Olympics might be possible four or five years after graduation when I'd gained some solid work experience. Instead, a series of events fell into place six months after convocation, and I landed a job with a small Canadian company specializing in uniforms for Olympic sponsors. I initially worked out of the Calgary office, supporting the Turin team for the 2006 Winter Games. Following Turin, we moved our offices to Vancouver in preparation for the Beijing 2008 and Vancouver 2010 Games.

The job was not quite as glamorous as you might imagine, but it had its perks: living abroad, attending some of the world's best sporting events and parties, watching the highest-caliber athletes of our time perform, and working alongside some of the top brands in the world. A little sexier than, say, mortgages—and it came with a stable and reliable pay cheque.

When I moved back to Vancouver, it was clear that something had to change with my living arrangements. My brother had purchased a one-bedroom condo with the help of my parents, which my sister and I rented from him, sharing to save costs. I suggested that I take it over: less stress for him, a good investment for me and an opportunity to have my own space.

We started by going to the bank where he had his mortgage to see if we could transfer the mortgage to my name. My mom suggested I see her mortgage broker for another option, which I did. I also visited my bank to see if there was a possibility of structuring the purchase to pay out some of my student loans in the process.

As my brother was willing to sell for less than the appraised value, my bank's mortgage approval meant I could repay him and my mom for their investment in the condo and say goodbye to some higher interest student debt at the same time. My mom's broker encouraged me to go with the bank's offer, which he felt was the best available.

In June 2006, I became a homeowner for the first time, with a mortgage of $176,256, at 5.1% interest on a four-year term with a 25-year **amortization**. Me and my first property on Oxford Street—it was meant to be.

Not long after, disaster struck. In late 2006, a large pipe sprung a leak, going unnoticed long enough that mold grew between the walls of my bathroom and my neighbour's unit. All the adjacent walls had to be removed and reinsulated. Fortunately, the pipes were considered strata property, and so the damage was covered under the strata's insurance.

I chose to see this mishap as an opportunity to upgrade. I could pay for a new bathtub, sink and toilet, and the cost of the labour, new flooring and tiles were covered by the insurance.

It meant not having a working bathroom for some time, so I moved in with my mom and sister. That meant it also made sense to do other upgrades as well, including new paint, flooring and closet fixtures. I painted the kitchen cupboards and added a new faucet and hardware. I hired my brother to help with the floors and a carpenter friend to remove a cupboard unit, opening the wall between the kitchen and the living and dining area.

With very little investment, my little East Van abode was quickly becoming a personal treasure for me—and I was building home equity in the process by increasing its potential sale value.

After working all day in my office, I worked on the renovations. Then I walked to my mom's home to sleep, often strolling through the well-known Main and Hastings intersection well after midnight. Some thought I was crazy, but this was my labour of love. It wasn't perfect, but it was a start.

LINGO!

AMORTIZATION AND TERM

Your mortgage *term* is the length of time your agreement with the lender covers, most commonly five years. The *amortization*, on the other hand, is the length of time it would take you to completely pay off your mortgage at the current rate of interest and payment schedule.

High-ratio borrowers (those whose down payment is less than 20% of the value of the home) are limited to 25-year amortizations.

For conventional mortgages (those with down payments of 20% or more of the value of the home), amortizations of 25 years or less can make it possible to access lower interest rates. However, if lower payments are desired, 30-year and, in rare situations, 35-year amortizations may be requested.

In most cases, I recommend choosing the longest amortization offered by the lender. The longer the amortization, the lower the payments. This is an important option. Job loss, illness and surprising housing costs like the unexpected need for a new furnace can put pressure on your monthly budget.

While your mortgage agreement will almost always allow you to make higher payments (more on this later) the option to revert to the lower required payments—or to extend your amortization back to its original length—can provide welcome options during tough times.

*If you want to pay off the mortgage quickly, using the lender's **prepayment privileges** to increase your payments or make lump-sum payments has the same effect as starting with a shorter amortization, without limiting your flexibility.*

28

PREPAYMENT PRIVILEGES

Many mortgages feature the option of making extra lump-sum payments or increased payments, without penalty. These features are usually referred to as prepayment privileges.

Lenders commonly offer the flexibility to pay between 10% and 25% (or more) over your regular payments. Some lenders may also offer skip-a-payment, miss-a-payment or double-up payment options. It's important to pay attention to this feature when choosing a mortgage—even just increasing your monthly payment by a few dollars or using your tax refund as a prepayment can shave time and interest costs off your mortgage.

Some lenders limit prepayments to once a year on the anniversary date, with minimum payments of $1,000. Others allow for lump-sum payments on any payment date with $100 minimums.

Most lenders also offer accelerated bi-weekly or accelerated weekly payments, which can reduce amortizations by two to 3.5 years over a five-year term..

Now it's your turn again.

For most Canadians, the "property ladder" looks something like this:

RUNG 1	**First home or rental home purchase** The primary aim here is usually to own a home, but it can also be to own property that is likely to increase in value, preparing the way for future purchases. *I recommend that my clients think of their first purchase as a future rental property. If you buy property with rental potential (desirable location, close to amenities and shopping, transit access, etc.), it may ease the pressure of feeling you need to find a "perfect" first property.*
RUNG 2	**First family home purchase** While it's clearly no longer 1960, most young Canadians still aspire to some form of their own family, even if it consists of a partner and a Labradoodle. The equity built in their first property can help them purchase a home suitable for two or more. Traditionally, this was the first rung on the property ladder, but with more marriages and other partnerships being delayed until later in life, this is often rung #2 these days.
RUNG 3	**First aspirational home purchase** You've built some equity, and it's time to move up, either to a more attractive neighbourhood or a more attractive home. You might be moving for work, perhaps even to another city. Or it could be to meet your growing family's need for more space or access to schools, extra-curricular activities or childcare. Or all of the above.
RUNG 4	**First rental property, second home or vacation property** You've built more equity and you're ready to invest it in more lifestyle (a vacation property) or more wealth-building potential (an investment/rental property).

RUNG 5	**Family dream home purchase** Life has been good to you, you've worked hard, and you've accumulated enough equity and income potential to make your dream affordable.
RUNG 6	**First downsized home** Life goes on, and your kids, if you had them, have now left the nest, leaving empty rooms behind. You may just be tired of the gardening and upkeep. It's time to simplify a bit and perhaps recapture some of the equity you've built for the retirement years ahead.
RUNG 7	**Retirement home** Job one: relax and enjoy life. Paid employment is now a thing of the past, and you want to be where you can fulfill your retirement dreams. It may even be time to start thinking about your proximity to things like health-care facilities.
RUNG 8	**Elder-years home** You need a bit more help now, and it's time to move to somewhere it's easy to access.

Of course, there are lots of ways to reinvent this path and make it your own. As you will read, Mark and I took our own unique trail.

In *Lean In: Women, Work and the Will to Lead*, Sheryl Sandberg titled one of her chapters "It's a Jungle Gym, Not a Ladder," referring to the corporate ladder. The same can be said of the property ladder. There is more than one way to get to your ideal milestones. Where you want to be and how you get there is unique to you. You may want to go straight to the tiny house on the lake lot and make that home for a lifetime. Or you might leap right into building a rental property portfolio.

Whatever your dreams for homeownership, this a great time to think about where you are now and where you want to be in the future.

Where do you live? What is it like? What is great about it? What could be improved?

Where do you want to be in 18 months? What do you hope to have accomplished in terms of your property goals?

Where do you want to be five years from now? Can you describe what it will look like, what you envision? The more details you include, the more powerful your vision will be.

What about 25 years from now? Can you imagine owning a home or even multiple properties, free and clear? What would that mean to you—and is it something you want?

If you don't own now and want to, what do you think you need to do to get there? If you own and want to upgrade or add more properties to your portfolio, what do you think you need to achieve that? (Think of these items as your initial action steps.)

Step 1

Step 2

Step 3

Step 4

Step 5

CHAPTER 4
To Step Forward, First Look Back

There are few experiences more disheartening than finding a place you want and then finding out it's not within your reach. To save yourself from this unnecessary suffering, talk to a mortgage broker before you start looking. We can help you understand your financing parameters as well as identify any potential challenges and create a plan to overcome them.

There are six core (and important) factors that determine whether your mortgage application will be approved.

1. Credit
2. Income
3. Down payment
4. Product and rates
5. Property type
6. Property use

Since there is much to cover for each of these, to make it a little easier to digest, I've divided these six core factors into three segments: the *past*, the *present*, and the *future*.

PAST	PRESENT	FUTURE
• Credit • Income	• Down payment • Product and rate	• Property type • Property use

The *past* is *what it is*. Much like taking a photo, it's a snapshot of your financial position. Click, the picture is captured and the foundation for your mortgage approval is based on what you have done up to this point—how you've used and managed your liabilities (credit) and how you've earned a living (income).

The *present* provides opportunity for choices in your investment and considerations for your return on investment (ROI): how much you want to invest (down payment), what product options and terms will align with your plans and how that is being influenced in the market today (product and rate).

Finally, the *future* is all about the property and how it will serve you and the lender now and in the coming years (property type and use).

Warning: we are jumping right into the depths of mortgages here. The next three chapters cover the foundations of a mortgage approval. Be prepared—the content can be dry and perhaps a bit boring, but it's the information that will be the most important to know and understand. If you can apply the knowledge presented, you can position yourself for the best borrowing potential now and in the future—which can have a substantial impact on your overall net worth.

This chapter, a beast of a chapter, features the two most significant factors related to your mortgage approval, your credit and your income, both of which are represented by reviewing your past.

THE PAST
Are you "creditworthy?"

Your credit score is *vital* for mortgage approval. It will determine the lender, product options and the rates available to you.

PAST

- Credit
- Income

39

The credit score is a rating given to individuals based on their borrowing habits. It's part of the **credit report**, which is basically the borrower's financial report card, an imprint of the past that cannot always be easily or quickly changed.

Increasing your credit score is a process requiring effort and attention, especially if your current score is not strong.

LINGO!

CREDIT REPORT

A financial report card that creditors use to determine creditworthiness for loan applications. These are generated and accessed through Equifax Canada or TransUnion Canada, who refer to credit reports as credit file disclosures or consumer disclosures, respectively.

Your credit score is one reason it is important to connect with a mortgage broker as soon as you start to think about buying or refinancing. A broker can help you review and, if necessary, improve your score to maximize your borrowing options.

Monitoring and keeping your score strong will make your life easier and save you money.

You may have heard that "cash is king." However, even if you're not swimming in money, you can take pride in having a "clean, thick and mature" credit report that entitles you to VIP privileges when it comes to borrowing. (Yes, **credit bureaus** do use terms like "clean, thick and mature" to describe your credit behaviour.)

LINGO!

CREDIT BUREAU

An agency that collects account information from various creditors to create reports on individual borrowing and payment habits. The major credit bureaus in Canada are Equifax Canada and TransUnion Canada.

UNDERSTANDING THE CREDIT REPORT

When a broker or lender pulls your credit report from a credit bureau (Equifax or TransUnion), the document will verify who you are, where you have lived and the jobs you've had. This is also why it is critical that you provide complete and accurate information in a mortgage application. Misrepresented information is a red flag to mortgage brokers and lenders.

For each debt, which we refer to in the industry as a "trade line," your report will also show when the account was established, when the last payment was made and whether it is still active or has been closed.

The report gives a brief synopsis of your credit use. Then it cryptically tells a story about how you have paid and managed debts through a list of letters and numbers (see below). The letters R, I, M, S, O, and C describe the type of debt (for each trade line) and the numbers 0 through 9 represent the payment history on that particular debt. The highest score, one (1), indicates that the borrower pays within 30 days of the payment due date. At nine (9) the debt is considered "bad" and is placed with a collection agency, which is not good.

R. Revolving credit, such as a credit card.
Payment amount changes based on outstanding balance.

I. Instalment loan, such as a student loan or car loan.
There is a set payment schedule established.

M. Mortgage

S. Lease

O. Open credit

C. Line of credit

1. The highest rating; borrower pays within 30 days of the payment due date.
2. Number of days the account is overdue. 30 days late.
3. 60 days late.
4. 90 days late.
5. 120 days late—and so on, through to collections at 9.

For a mortgage, **M4** (not M9) means the account is in or near foreclosure. A letter of demand will usually be issued by this point. You *never* want to miss a mortgage payment if you can help it! If it happens or is inevitable, you must get on it immediately to rectify. Call me or your mortgage broker if you need help. This is vital.

Delay in Reporting

Each of your creditors (trade lines) report your account status (the type of debt and payment rating) to Equifax and TransUnion. These updates are reported at various times, so your outstanding balance and payment amount may not be current on the date the credit report is pulled. Those details can be adjusted in the mortgage application if it's necessary.

Credit Challenged

If you have had late accounts, accounts that were written off or are in collections, or if you have filed for consumer proposal or bankruptcy, there are other things you need to consider before buying a home. There may be a delay before you can get a mortgage or you may have to consider alternative lender options, with higher rates and fees.

No Credit

If you have no credit history, the results can be the same as having a very bad score. If you are planning to have a mortgage in the future, ensure you open at least two reputable credit accounts to start building your score immediately.

Mobile Providers Can Hurt. They Don't Help.

Many people think only about their credit card and loan accounts when considering their credit history and are shocked to learn their score has been affected by a missed final payment on a cellphone bill that went astray when they changed mobile providers. An unpaid cell phone bill of a few hundred dollars is not worth the potential future costs of paying higher interest rates and mortgage fees in the thousands of dollars.

For this reason alone, it is essential to check your score at least once a year and follow up on any mishaps. Anything reported to Equifax or TransUnion has the potential to impact your score, good or bad.

Furthermore, a cell phone bill does not necessarily count as a reputable trade line for lenders. They want to see established credit resources (borrowed funds) that are managed well.

Experiencing Hardship

If you have not yet missed a payment and are experiencing hardship or divorce or are in a situation where you can't meet your debt obligations, contact me or your broker so a plan can be put in place with your lender to lower the chances of it damaging your credit score or forcing a potential foreclosure.

Dealing with challenging times at the onset is always easier and more effective than trying to fix the problem later.

Consumer Proposal or Bankruptcy

If you are considering a consumer proposal or bankruptcy, this has the potential to impact future homeownership. Even though they say bankruptcy only appears on the credit bureau reports for seven years, there are trails left and a lender can always spot them. Be aware that this is a decision that is likely to affect you for the life of your credit history.

Errors Are Common

It is common for there to be errors or inaccurate reports from the bureaus. It is much easier and less stressful to deal with these issues when you are not in the midst of needing a mortgage approval.

Believe me, it can be a major hassle if you need to make updates with a specific creditor while trying to get a mortgage approval—a major hassle that could even lead to losing an opportunity to buy a home you want or being declined for a mortgage altogether.

MONITORING YOUR CREDIT SCORE

You can sign up online for a subscription with Equifax to get regular updates on your credit. The subscription includes identity theft insurance. If you don't want to pay the monthly fee, you can purchase an individual report or request one free Equifax and TransUnion report each year, by mail. If you need to dispute inaccuracies, you can do so through the Equifax and TransUnion websites.

43

Subscription/Individual Reports:

Google: Equifax complete premier plan
Google: Equifax instant online snapshot
Google: TransUnion product disclosure

Equifax & TransUnion Free Report:

Google: Equifax free report by mail
Google: TransUnion free report by mail

Equifax and TransUnion Credit Report Dispute:

Google: Equifax disputes
Google: TransUnion disputes

For further details on how to read and understand your consumer credit score, read the Equifax Consumer Credit Report User Guide: *google: Equifax Consumer User Guide Canada.*

MAXIMIZING YOUR CREDIT SCORE

A better score can mean a better mortgage, potentially saving you money and stress. Clients known in the industry as "**high ratio**," those with less than 20% for their down payment, have a minimum credit score requirement of 600. **Conventional mortgage** borrowers, those with more than 20% for their down payment, are subject to lender discretion on minimum credit scores. Most lenders want applicants to have a score of at least 650. Additional perks may be available with credit scores higher than 680, with further specials for applicants with scores over 700 and 800.

LINGO!

HIGH-RATIO MORTGAGE

The down payment is less than 20% of the value or purchase price. Put another way, these mortgages have a **loan-to-value (LTV)** higher than 80%.

Mortgage default insurance will be required, with premiums paid by the borrower. Premiums are usually wrapped in to the mortgage and amortized with the loan.

CONVENTIONAL MORTGAGE

The down payment is more than 20% of the value or purchase price. Put another way, these mortgages have a loan-to-value of less than 80%.

LOAN-TO-VALUE (LTV)

The ratio of a loan to the value or purchase price.

Examples:

$$\text{High-Ratio LTV} = \frac{\$475,000 \text{ loan amount}}{\$500,000 \text{ purchase price}} = 95\%$$

$$\text{Conventional LTV} = \frac{\$400,000 \text{ loan amount}}{\$500,000 \text{ purchase price}} = 80\%$$

MORTGAGE DEFAULT INSURANCE

Allows homebuyers to purchase a home with less than 20% towards the down payment. The borrower pays a premium based on the loan-to-value of the purchase. This can be paid as a lump-sum amount or more commonly included and amortized with the mortgage. The insurance protects the lender should a borrower default on the loan.

It's not just making payments on time that determines your score. Long-standing accounts, the number of accounts you have, maintaining lower balances and regular use, among other things, are all factors.

The following is a review of good credit management practices that can protect you from future grief. Under each guideline is space for you to write down any notes about the credit you have or issues you may have had and any action steps you need to take to get back on track. This exercise will help you have an informed conversation with your mortgage broker and provide a framework for improvement if needed. To get you started, a chart is provided to list the liabilities you (and your partner, if applicable) are currently managing.

Don't skip this essential step—your future self will thank you!

45

LIABILITIES LIST

DEBT	STARTED (YEAR)	INTEREST RATE	LIMIT	OUTSTANDING BALANCE	MONTHLY PAYMENT
(Example 1) Credit Card	2011	19.99%	$5,000	$750	$25
(Example 2) Car Loan	2012	5.50%	$25,000	$4,750	$408
		TOTAL			

GOOD CREDIT MANAGEMENT PRACTICES

1. Pay your bills on time.

Delinquent payments and collections can have a significant negative impact on your score. Always pay your bills on time. Try to pay your bill in full. If you cannot pay in full, then at least make the minimum monthly payment noted on your statement before your due date.

_____

_____

_____

_____

2. Stay current with payments and pay off debt.

If you have missed payments, get current and stay current. If you own a home and your debts are compounding and becoming unmanageable, consider a debt consolidation plan through a refinance before your credit score is damaged. This can also provide interest savings and simplify monthly payments. If you don't own, reviewing your debts and consolidating in another way may be beneficial. It's better to consider these options before your credit is hurt by missed payments. Talk to a financial planner and mortgage broker to set a plan for debt consolidation.

_____

_____

_____

_____

3.   Understand and know your score.

According to Equifax, your credit score is based on five factors with weighted importance, including payment history (35%), your used credit vs your available credit (30%), type of credit you have (15%), new credit (10-12%) and the length of your credit history (5-7%). Knowing what the bureaus track and their importance, will help you make strong intelligent decisions on your credit.

NOTE: Your consumer score will vary slightly from the financial score pulled by a mortgage broker or lender. The algorithms have different weighted averages, which produce slightly different scores. Equifax and TransUnion will also report varying scores.

4.   Manage your accounts wisely.

Apply for and open new credit accounts only as needed. Use credit cards and lines of credit frequently, but manage them responsibly. If you need to re-establish your credit history, opening new accounts, use them for your basic purchases and pay them off each month.

5. Maintain at least two reputable credit accounts.

In general, major credit cards (Visa, MasterCard and American Express) and/or a line of credit or instalment loans (such as a car loan) with a well-known financial institution are more favourable for your credit score than, say, a department store credit card or less-known credit companies. Always maintain at least two reputable credit accounts. Cell phone providers report to the bureaus—they do not have a positive influence to a lender; however, they can have a negative impact if payments are missed.

6. Keep balances low.

Keep your balances low on credit cards and other revolving credit, and never go over the limit. The rule of thumb is to keep balances at or below 50% of your limit. If you are working on re-establishing your credit or want the highest possible score, keep daily balances below 30% of your approved limit on all revolving credit accounts.

7.   Consider the number of credit inquiries.

The Equifax Risk Score distinguishes between a search for a single loan and a search for many new credit lines, partly by the length of time over which inquiries occur and by who is pulling them. Using a broker when you're shopping for a mortgage allows for one credit inquiry to be used for multiple lenders.

8.   Cautiously open new accounts.

Avoid opening new credit accounts unnecessarily or applying for multiple credit cards in a brief period (if you already have established credit). Either could have a negative effect on your credit score.

Remember—the length of your credit history matters. If you are a new user, set up a couple of strong accounts to start, such as a Visa or Master-Card and a line of credit from your bank.

9.   Think twice about closing unused credit cards or loans.

If you have had an account for years but are not using it, closing it can have a negative effect on your credit score as the account's history is likely favourable.

10.   Finally—when you're ready to apply for a mortgage, maintain strong credit habits through to closing.

A lender may request a new credit bureau before your **closing date**. If your score has dropped, that could change the status of your approval, impact the interest rate or even mean the lender can't fund the mortgage.

IMPORTANT! Do not open new accounts or make large purchases requiring financing if a mortgage application has been submitted to a lender for approval, or if you already have a mortgage approval waiting to close.

Always review with your mortgage broker first before adding new credit or loans if you are in the process of buying or refinancing.

Adding additional debt following your original application could cause the lender to terminate their approval and leave you without a mortgage on your closing date.

LINGO!

CLOSING DATE

The purchase or refinance date—the day the purchase and sale take place and/or the money changes hands. If you have a mortgage, this is the day the loan funds will be released by the lender to complete the purchase or refinance transaction.

THE PAST
Your Income

Lenders assume that the income you earn in the future will be similar to the income you've earned in the past, so income is assessed by looking at past earnings.

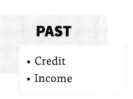

PAST

- Credit
- Income

53

When it comes to a mortgage approval, how you make your money is just as important as how much you make. Employment salary, salary with bonus, salary with bonus and allowances, commission, self-employment sole proprietor, self-employed incorporated, part-time, RRIFs, pension, spousal support, etc.—all require different kinds of verification. Further, different lenders may require different documentation, may have different policies and may use different calculations for the types and amounts of income used.

WHEN YOU HAVE A JOB (EMPLOYED)

For a regular salaried employee, most lenders will request two or more of the following: a letter of employment, recent pay stub, deposit of pay into a bank account, T4s and recent notice of assessment (NOA) documents from the Canada Revenue Agency (CRA).

The letter of employment, on official letterhead, must include your name, position, the length of time you've been employed, your salary along with any bonuses or allowances, and contact details of the person signing the letter so that the lender can confirm the details verbally. If you are paid hourly, the hourly wage and *guaranteed* number of hours per week need to be noted.

The pay stub verifies that you are still working and that your year-to-date (YTD) income aligns with the employment salary. If there is a reason the YTD amount is lower or higher, provide it to your broker, who can acknowledge it to the lender. For example, perhaps you took extended holidays without pay, took medical or maternity leave, worked on a big project with extensive overtime or got a raise part way through the year.

If needed, confirmation of the deposit into a bank account is further validation that you are still employed and that your income is in line with the current pay stub.

IMPORTANT! Maternity leave will be assessed differently by each lender. Some will account for a percentage of income made previously (~60%) while others will allow for 100% of income if the applicant can provide a letter of employment with a return-to-work date.

The notice of assessment verifies there are no taxes outstanding to CRA. If there are, the lender will want verification that these have been paid before they consider approval. A lender does not want to be in second position behind CRA for any amount of money, as this can potentially impact the security of the loan. Verification can be made by providing a statement of account available from CRA or by showing your payment made through your bank.

NOTE: If you cannot find a copy of your NOA, you or your accountant may have online access to your CRA account to get a copy, or you can call 1-800-959-8281 and request a copy to be mailed to you. If you have online banking set up, CRA may be able to email this to you for immediate access.

T4s help to support income verification if there are bonuses, other benefits, part-time employment or other considerations to factor. You are usually asked to provide a two-year T4 history, especially if an average income needs to be calculated.

WHEN YOU OWN A BUSINESS (SELF-EMPLOYED)

If you are self-employed, referred to as business-for-self (BFS) in the industry, the documents required include your T1 Generals (your tax returns) for two years (possibly, in some rare cases, three years), including the statement of business activities, and your NOA for the past two years. The T1 can be a lengthy document, and yes, the FULL document must be provided. If the business is incorporated, a business license or notice of articles may also be requested to verify that the business is and has been operational for more than two years.

Since self-employed income can fluctuate from year to year, lenders want to see a minimum two-year tax history. This could mean you need to be in business for three years to show two years of completed taxes. There can be exceptions made, but the reasoning needs to be convincing.

Typically, lenders will average the two-year history if income is increasing. If the income is decreasing year-over-year, the lender may only use the most recent year's income. Lenders are specifically looking at line 150 on the T1 and NOA for the income used. **55**

The T1 gives a detailed overview of the income earned and any associated write-offs for the business. For proprietorships, depending on the business and the types of write-offs, a lender may approve "add-backs." This gives the borrower the ability to add the cost of certain write-offs (business use of your home, capital cost allowance, motor vehicle expense, depreciation and amortization of equipment) back into income. This can be substantial, particularly if expensive equipment or tools are required to operate the business.

Another possibility with BFS files is a term we call "gross-up." This allows non-incorporated clients such as sole proprietors to gross up their earnings (line 150 on the T1) by 15% to account for some of the write-offs deducted from their income.

Since business owners have many write-offs and try to keep most of the income in the business by paying themselves sparingly, there are other mortgage programs and options available to BFS applicants if they are not able to qualify with the standard guidelines. The stated income program (discussed on page 187) provides a BFS buyer the option to "state" his or her income within reason for qualification purposes.

For the same reason as the salaried employee, the BFS applicant must produce the NOA to confirm no taxes are owing to CRA and to verify two years of income.

LENDERS

Income and credit will play a role in the type of lender a mortgage file can be submitted to for approval.

There are basically three lender tiers:

1. **A lenders**
2. **B lenders**
3. **Private lenders**

A lenders offer best market rates to A borrowers. B and private lenders can provide decent alternative lending options if the borrower does not meet the minimum A standards, has damaged credit or does not have sufficient income to qualify under the standard debt ratios, or if the property has some unique factors that will not be approved by A lenders.

LINGO!

A LENDERS

Bank, **credit union** and **monoline** lenders, offering their best rates and products to A clients with good credit, qualified income and resources for down payment.

BANK

A financial institution that accepts deposits from the public and creates credit. Lending activities can be performed either directly or indirectly through capital markets.

Of the top five banks in Canada, two use the broker channel, Scotiabank and TD Canada Trust. The other top banks do not currently lend directly through brokers, but they are usually large investors in monoline lenders within the broker channel. Many other banks are part of the broker channel including, but not limited to: B2B, Bridgewater, CFF, Equitable, ICICI, Manulife and Street Capital.

Banks are regulated by the Office of the Superintendent of Financial Institutions (OSFI) and the Bank Act, so their products and mortgage specialists do not always have the same guidelines to follow as credit unions and mortgage brokers regulated by the Financial Institutions Commission (FICOM). Bank mortgage officers (sometimes known as mortgage specialists, representatives, advisers or advisors), are not required to complete a mortgage licensing course.

CREDIT UNION

Their products, services and operations resemble those offered by banks, but there are some differences. Specifically, they are made up of a membership; they are locally owned and invest their profits in the communities where they operate and where their members live and work.

Credit unions are regulated by FICOM. With the members as owners, there can be cases where it is more difficult to get an approval, but sometimes they can be more flexible if the client is an existing member. Due to their slightly different regulations and operations, they have unique programs that can sometimes provide more borrowing power or different qualification options.

With most lenders' products, you can port your mortgage to a new home when you move as long as you requalify. This includes inter-provincial moves. With credit unions, porting your mortgage may be restricted to your current area and you may not be able to port intra-provincially. If your career has a high probability for relocation, a credit union mortgage may not be the best option.

MONOLINE LENDER (MORTGAGE FINANCING COMPANY)

These companies focus solely on mortgages or mortgage-like products secured by real estate. They do not operate storefront locations like the major banks and credit unions. This lowers overhead expenses and the saving can be passed on to borrowers through discounted interest rates.

Monolines also offer unique and flexible mortgage products not available through banks or credit unions and often have lower payout penalties should a borrower break the mortgage contract before maturity.

Although you may not be familiar with monoline lenders' brand names, many have been in the industry for decades and have billions of dollars in residential and commercial financing.

As they don't have storefront locations, they focus on their online and phone customer service presence. For example, First National is repeatedly recognized for their "My Mortgage" client portal, which is one of the most efficient mortgage management systems in the industry. From checking mortgage balances to taking advantage of prepayment privileges, clients can manage one of their most important investments right from their home.

B LENDER (ALTERNATIVE LENDER)

These lenders offer a variety of mortgage products aimed at clients who may be missing income verification or a strong credit history, or who may have been through a consumer proposal or bankruptcy.

B lenders usually require a down payment of at least 15%. Their interest rates are generally 1% to 3% higher than market rates, with upfront fees of 1% to 3% of the mortgage amount borrowed. Terms offered are usually one to three years.

B lending is ideally a short-term solution to improve a borrower's position so they can convert to an A lender in the future. B lenders like to know the exit plan for the client and how they plan to improve their situation.

B lenders help many families get back on their feet during credit challenges or life events that put them in short-term hardship. They also offer unique options for borrowers that don't necessarily fit into the A lender's boxes at the time.

PRIVATE LENDER

Private lenders can be individuals or companies known as mortgage investment corporations (MICs). Private lenders are unregulated and therefore do not have to abide by rules set by the provincial or federal governments.

They are mainly interested in the property. The borrower's credit or income may not play a significant role. The lender will review both to get an overall feel for the applicant, but it is the property (location, resale potential and equity) that is important.

Private lenders will consider unique properties as well as offer more flexible options for borrowers requiring construction financing. However, they charge higher interest rates (usually 4% to 10% higher than market rates). They typically want to see a minimum of 35% investment from the borrower.

There are also upfront fees ranging from 2% to 5% of the mortgage amount, but some private lenders charge a higher interest rate with no fees or penalties. Payments are most commonly interest-only with 12-month terms. The lender is hoping to be a short-term solution for the borrower, but usually will have renewal options if payments have been consistent.

INCOME DOCUMENTATION

The charts that follow cover the income documents that are usually requested by traditional A lenders. Samples are also provided.

B lenders may have different requirements for income verification, which will be specific to each file.

Private lenders usually have minimal document requirements, which, again, will be file specific.

NOTE: Lender's requests and government documents can change frequently, so follow up with your mortgage broker to ensure you have the most recent and up-to-date documents list.

INCOME DOCUMENT REQUIREMENTS
Employee

SALARIED/HOURLY EMPLOYED DOCUMENTATION	NOTES
Two Most Recent Pay Stubs	Lender may request to see deposit of pay into account.
Letter of Employment (LOE)	Must be dated within 30 days of: 1. Accepted offer to purchase, or 2. Application for renewal or refinance. The letter must include applicant's name, position, tenure, salary (or hourly wage and guaranteed hours) and note any overtime/bonus option, if applicable. It should be on company letterhead and signed by author (owner, manager or HR representative) including contact details. Lender will call for verbal confirmation of employment.
Most recent Notice of Assessment (NOA)	Need to show no taxes owing. If taxes owed, must provide proof of outstanding taxes paid. *note the tax year, not the mailing date
T4	1. Most recent T4 if income is salary 2. Two (2) most recent T4s if any income is commissioned, part-time, overtime, bonus or any additional benefits such as car allowance.

INCOME DOCUMENT REQUIREMENTS
Self-Employed

BUSINESS-FOR-SELF DOCUMENTATION	NOTES
2 most recent T1 Generals	Third party (accountant) completed taxes inclusive of Statement of Business Activities.
2 most recent Notice of Assessments	Need to show no taxes owing. If taxes owed, must provide proof of outstanding taxes paid.
Business License	If applicable, two-year history.
Notice of Articles	If applicable, it demonstrates the shareholders of the company.

SAMPLE: INCOME DOCUMENT
Pay Stub

THE MOST PROFITABLE BUSINESS

PAYMENT DATE:

PAY END DATE:

STATEMENT OF EARNINGS AND DEDUCTIONS

EARNINGS	DATE YMMDD	RATE	CURRENT HRS/UNITS	CURRENT AMOUNT	YTD HRS/UNITS	YTD AMOUNT
REGULAR		0.0000	0.00	1625.50	0.00	30785.00
RRSP		0.0000	0.00	32.50	0.00	617.50
TXBUFEF		0.0000	0.00	5.94	0.00	112.86
TOTAL EARNINGS				1663.44		31605.36
LESS TAXABLE BENEFITS				38.44		730.36
TOTAL GROSS				1625.00		30875.00

DEDUCTIONS	CURRENT AMOUNT	YTD AMOUNT	DEDUCTIONS	CURRENT AMOUNT	YTD AMOUNT
GOVT PEN	75.12	1427.28	EI CONT	29.50	560.50
FEDL TAX	248.52	4683.88	R.R.S.P.	32.50	617.50
LTD	18.12	344.28			
TOTAL DEDUCTIONS				401.76	7633.44

NET PAY 1223.24

NON NEGOTIABLE

SAVINGS ACCT:

DEND. DEP. ACCT:

EMPL./PAYEE ID.: 30AB 001

OCCUPATION: ADVISOR

NO. PAY PER.: 19 OF 24

CONFIDENTIAL

30AB 001

JOHN SMITH

NET PAY: $***1223.24

NOTIFICATION OF DEPOSIT TO ACCT: 12 XXXXXXXX1234

SAMPLE: INCOME DOCUMENT
Notice of Assessment

	Canada Revenue Agency	Agence du revenu du Canada		Protected B internal use only

SURREY BC V3T 5E1

0136560

Page 1

Notice details

Social insurance number	111 111 111
Tax year	2015
Date issued	March 03, 2016
Tax centre	City PROV POSTAL CODE

NAME NAME
1234 STREET NAME
CITY PROV   POSTAL CODE

BB583LZ4

Notice of assessment

We assessed your 2015 income tax and benefit return and calculated your balance.

You need to pay **$9,837.10.**

To avoid additional interest charges please pay by **April 30, 2016.**

Thank you,

Andrew Treusch
Commissioner of Revenue

Account summary

You have an amount due. If you already paid the full amount, please ignore this request.

Amount due:	$9,837.10
Pay by:	April 30, 2016

Payment options

You can:
- pay online
- pay at your financial institution

For more information, see page 5.

T451 E (16)

Canada

SAMPLE: INCOME DOCUMENT
Letter of Employment (LOE)

PRIVATE & CONFIDENTIAL

RE: Letter of Employment

(Date)

To Whom It May Concern:

This letter is to confirm that (employee name) is an employee of (company name). (Employee name) has been employed with our Company since (start date).

Presently, (employee name) is working full-time as a (position), earning an annual salary of (salary amount).

Please do not hesitate to contact me directly should you require further information.

Regards,

(Contact's Signature)

(Contact Name)
(Contact's Title/Position)
Tel:
Email:
Address:

IRENE STRONG | rex-a@irenestrong.com
Mortgage Professional | 778 547 8466
@irene_strong

SAMPLE: INCOME DOCUMENT

T4

Employer's name — Nom de l'employeur

Canada Revenue Agency
Agence du revenu du Canada

Year
Année

T4

Statement of Remuneration Paid
État de la rémunération payée

Employment income – line 101
Revenus d'emploi – ligne 101

14

Income tax deducted – line 437
Impôt sur le revenu retenu – ligne 437

22

Protected B when completed / Protégé B une fois rempli

54 Employer's account number / Numéro de compte de l'employeur

Province of employment
Province d'emploi

10

Employee's CPP contributions – line 308
Cotisations de l'employé au RPC – ligne 308

16

EI insurable earnings
Gains assurables d'AE

24

Social insurance number
Numéro d'assurance sociale

12

Exempt – Exemption
CPP/QPP   EI   PPIP

28

RPC/RRQ AE RPAP

Employment code
Code d'emploi

29

Employee's QPP contributions – line 308
Cotisations de l'employé au RRQ – ligne 308

17

CPP/QPP pensionable earnings
Gains ouvrant droit à pension – RPC/RRQ

26

Employee's name and address – Nom et adresse de l'employé

Last name (in capital letters) – Nom de famille (en lettres moulées)   First name – Prénom   Initial – Initiale

Employee's EI premiums – line 312
Cotisations de l'employé à l'AE – ligne 312

18

Union dues – line 212
Cotisations syndicales – ligne 212

44

RPP contributions – line 207
Cotisations à un RPA – ligne 207

20

Charitable donations – line 349
Dons de bienfaisance – ligne 349

46

Pension adjustment – line 206
Facteur d'équivalence – ligne 206

52

RPP or DPSP registration number
N° d'agrément d'un RPA ou d'un RPDB

50

Employee's PPIP premiums – see over
Cotisations de l'employé au RPAP – voir au verso

55

PPIP insurable earnings
Gains assurables du RPAP

56

Other information (see over)	Box – Case	Amount – Montant	Box – Case	Amount – Montant	Box – Case	Amount – Montant
Autres renseignements (voir au verso)	Box – Case	Amount – Montant	Box – Case	Amount – Montant	Box – Case	Amount – Montant

T4 (17)

SAMPLE: INCOME DOCUMENT
T1 General

SAMPLE: INCOME DOCUMENT
Business License

CITY OF VANCOUVER

LICENCES & INSPECTIONS DEPARTMENT
City Hall, East Wing
453 West 12th Avenue
Vancouver, BC. Canada V5Y 1V4
Within Vancouver Telephone: 3-1-1
Outside Vancouver: 604-873-7000

CITY OF
VANCOUVER

The Most Profitable Business
111 GRANVILLE ST Unit 123
Vancouver, BC CAN V5L 1K2

2011

Account #: 123456
Licence #: 11-223344

BUSINESS LICENCE
Issued Jul 05, 2011
Expires Dec 31, 2011

Business Licence Holder: The Most Profitable Business

Business Type:
Subtype: Other

Business Trade Name: The Most Profitable Business
Located At: 111 GRANVILLE ST Unit 123

Additional approvals may be required provincially or federally.

App Fee (Non-Refundable)	$50.00
Business Licence Fee	$124.00
Total Fee Paid:	$174.00

The above named, having paid the required fees, is hereby licensed to carry on the business, trade, profession or other occupation stated herein. This licence is issued subject to the provisions of all by-laws of the City of Vancouver now or hereafter in force and to all amendments that may hereafter, during the currency of this licence, be made to said by-laws. In issuing this licence the City does not represent or warrant compliance with other City of Vancouver by-laws. The licensee is responsible for ensuring compliance with all relevant by-laws of the City and additional approvals may be required provincially or federally. If this licence has been issued in conjunction with a time-limited Development Permit, this licence will not be valid if the Development Permit has expired and has not been extended. This licence must be posted upon the licensed premise and is valid at this address only.

SAMPLE: INCOME DOCUMENT
Notice of Articles

 **BRITISH COLUMBIA**
Ministry of Finance
Corporate and Personal
Property Registries

Number:

68

CERTIFICATE

OF

INCORPORATION

BUSINESS CORPORATIONS ACT

I Hereby Certify that **The Most Profitable Business** was incorporated under the Business Corporations Act of August 23, 2004 at 04:43 PM Pacific Time.

Issued under my hand at Victoria, British Columbia
On August 23, 2004

Registrar of Companies
Province of British Columbia
Canada

SAMPLE: INCOME DOCUMENT
Notice of Articles Cont'd

BRITISH
COLUMBIA

Ministry of Finance
Corporate and Personal
Property Registries
www.corporateonline.gov.bc.ca

Mailing Address:
PO BOX 9431 Stn prov Govt.
Victoria BC V8W 9V3

Location:
2nd Floor – 940 Blashard St.
Victoria BC
250 356-8626

Notice of Articles

CERTIFIED COPY
Of a document filed with the Province of
British Columbia Registrar of Companies

69

BUINESS CORPORATIONS ACT

This Notice of Articles was issued by the Registrar on: August 30, 2006 01:21 PM Pacific Time

Incorporation Number: **BC0000000**

Recognition Date and time: Incorporated on August 30, 2006 01:21 PM Pacific Time

NOTICE OF ARTICLES

Name of Company:

The most Profitable Business

REGISTERED OFFICE INFORMATION

Mailing Address:
111 GRANVILLE UNIT 123
VANCOUVER BC V5L 1K2
CANADA

Delivery Address:
111 GRANVILLE UNIT 123
VANCOUVER BC V5L 1K2
CANADA

RECORDS OFFICE INFORMATION

Mailing Address:
111 GRANVILLE UNIT 123
VANCOUVER BC V5L 1K2
CANADA

Delivery Address:
111 GRANVILLE UNIT 123
VANCOUVER BC V5L 1K2
CANADA

OTHER INCOME VERIFICATION

There are many other sources of income that lenders may consider. Some will be considered by all; others by only a few select lenders. Advise your mortgage broker of all income sources and provide verification documentation to see if, and how, it can be used. Below is a list of some common "other income" sources and their verification requirements:

INCOME DOCUMENT REQUIREMENTS
Other Income Sources

OTHER INCOME SOURCES	POTENTIAL VERIFICATION
Rental Income	1. T1 Generals showing statement of rental activities, or 2. Tenancy Agreement with a current 1-year lease, or 3. Appraisal with Schedule A (broker ordered) Along with the rental income, property details will also have to be verified with: • Recent mortgage statement • Recent property tax notice • Confirmation of strata fees, if needed
Child Support	• Court order for child support • Proof of age of child • Confirmation of deposits into account
Child Benefits	• T1 Generals or tax return confirmation • Proof of age of child • Confirmation of deposits into account
Investment Dividends	1. T1 Generals, 2. T5, or 3. Other confirmation sources
Permanent Disability	• Benefit letter from insurance company • Current pay stub • Confirmation of deposits into account
Pension	• Two year Notice of Assessment • Two years' T4s of all pension income (RIFs, OAS, CPP) • Direct deposit verification into account • Pension pay statement confirming benefits

CO-SIGNER OR GUARANTOR

Sometimes your income or credit may not be strong enough for the purchase you wish to make, but it may be possible to get approval with a **co-signer** or **guarantor** added to an application to strengthen the file.

LINGO!

CO-SIGNER

In cases where an applicant may not be able to be approved for a mortgage due to poor credit score or insufficient income verification, a co-signer can be added to the application. The co-signer will be on the title of the property but may not be required to live on the property.

GUARANTOR

In cases where an applicant may not be able to be approved for a mortgage mostly due to credit score, a guarantor supports the file with his or her credit. The guarantor will not be on the title or be considered an income contributor to the mortgage. A guarantor must usually be a spouse or immediate family member and reside on the property.

A guarantor may be the best alternative for an applicant (versus a co-signer) if the applicant wants to meet the qualifications for property transfer tax exemption or the BC HOME Partnership program (discussed further in Chapter 10).

Now you.

Make a note here of the documents you'll need to collect for your type of employment and other income streams:

INCOME	✓	NOTES
EMPLOYED		
2 recent Pay Stubs		
Letter of Employment		
Notice of Assessment		
2 most recent T4s		
SELF-EMPLOYED		
2 most recent T1 Generals (FULL doc)		
2 most recent Notice of Assessments		
Business Licence		
Notice of Articles		
OTHER INCOME		
Rental Income		
Child Support		
Child Benefits		
Investment Dividends		
Permanent Disability		
Pension		
Other		

Other points or income to address

- ....

- ....

- ....

DEBT RATIOS

To calculate the mortgage amount a borrower can qualify for, two debt ratios are used, **gross debt service ratio (GDS)** and **total debt service ratio (TDS)**.

LINGO!

GROSS DEBT SERVICE RATIO (GDS)

The percentage of the borrower's income needed to pay all required monthly housing costs (mortgage payments, property taxes, heat and 50% of condo fees).

TOTAL DEBT SERVICE RATIO (TDS)

The percentage of the borrower's income needed to cover housing costs (GDS) plus any other monthly obligations, such as credit card payments and car payments.

For insured mortgages, the *maximum* ratios are 39% GDS and 44% TDS for borrowers with credit scores higher than 680. Below 680, the GDS and TDS can be limited to 35% and 42% respectively. The minimum credit score required is 600. The BC HOME Partnership loan and loans with non-traditional down payment sources (borrowed funds) require a minimum score of 650.

For conventional mortgages, different lenders and products have varying degrees of allowable percentages, from 32% GDS and 40% TDS to no limit on GDS and exception bases on TDS up to 50% for special circumstances or very strong files with low loan-to-value (LTV). B lenders allow for TDS ratios of 45% to 50%, and private lenders do not usually look at debt ratios.

CALCULATING GDS AND TDS

Here's an example of how debt ratios are calculated:

Applicants with a combined annual income of $72,000 ($6,000 per month) want to buy a place for $500,000, with a $100,000 down payment. The property has annual taxes of $1,200, monthly strata fees of $300 and heating costs of $50. The applicants have a $400 monthly car loan payment and a $50 credit card payment. The mortgage they are applying for has an interest rate of 3.1% with a 30-year amortization, for monthly payments of $1,700 (principal plus interest).

74

GDS

$$= \frac{\text{Principal (P)+Interest (I)+Taxes+Strata (50\%)+Heat}}{\text{Gross Monthly Income}}$$

$$= \frac{\$1,700 \text{ (P+I)}+\$100 \text{ taxes}+\$150 \text{ strata}+\$50 \text{ heat}}{\$6,000 \text{ income}}$$

$$= \frac{\$2,000 \text{ housing costs}}{\$6,000 \text{ income}}$$

$= $ **33% GDS**

TDS

$$= \frac{\text{Principal (P)+Interest (I)+Taxes+Strata (50\%)+Heat+Other Debts}}{\text{Gross Monthly Income}}$$

$$= \frac{\$1,700 \text{ (P+I)}+\$100 \text{ taxes}+\$150 \text{ strata}+\$50 \text{ heat}+400 \text{ car}+\$50 \text{ credit}}{\$6,000 \text{ income}}$$

$$= \frac{\$2,450 \text{ housing costs}}{\$6,000 \text{ income}}$$

$= $ **41% TDS**

Assuming credit is good and their income and down payment can be verified, these clients should be approved for the $400,000 loan, with room to spare in their debt ratios.

> **IMPORTANT!** It's the monthly payments associated with debt that impact your affordability, not necessarily the total amount of debt. In today's market, roughly speaking, mortgage affordability will drop by *approximately $25,000 for every $100 in monthly payments*. For example, if applicants could qualify for a $400,000 mortgage but decided to get a new car with a $400 monthly payment, their mortgage affordability would decrease by $100,000 ($25,000 x 4) to approximately $300,000.

UNDERSTANDING HOW YOUR DEBT IS CALCULATED

Certain debts may require a calculated payment rather than the payment shown on your credit report.

Home Equity Line of Credit (HELOC)

Let's assume a **home equity line of credit (HELOC)** has a balance of $30,000 with interest-only payments of $86 per month. The lender will usually require the balance to be amortized over 25 years at the current **benchmark rate**. At today's rate, a payment of $173 would be included in the ratio calculations rather than the current $86 payment.

Line of Credit (LOC)

Lines of credit payments are also commonly adjusted. Many lenders include a payment equal to 3% of the balance. That same $30,000 in a line of credit debt would be calculated as a $900 monthly payment rather than the interest-only payment, which may only be around $175.

Paying Debts versus Down Payment

In some cases, therefore, it's sensible to use less of your savings for the down payment so that you can pay off certain debts and qualify for the higher mortgage amount if needed. This option also helps to consolidate debt payments and potentially lowers your overall interest costs. Note: in rare cases, the lender may require an account to be closed after payment is made.

Should debts need to be paid, lenders will want to see statements or the accounts showing a zero balance. In the case of a **refinance** to consolidate debt, it may be a condition of the approval that the debts are to be paid by the **solicitor** with the proceeds of the new mortgage. Recent statements, including name, account number and outstanding balance for each debt will need to be provided for the solicitor to make payment.

BC HOME Partnership Loan

The BC HOME Partnership Loan is another liability calculated separately by lenders. Even though the loan from the government is interest free for the first five years, lenders want to know the borrower can maintain the future debt, so the loan amount is amortized over 20 years at the benchmark rate. With a benchmark rate of 4.99%, a $10,000 BC HOME Partnership loan would be approximately a $65 monthly liability.

Student Loans

Student loans may also be treated differently by each lender. A general rule is that, if the loan is not yet in repayment, the payment is considered to be 1% of the outstanding balance. If the loan is in repayment, the instalment payment from the credit report is used.

LINGO!

HOME EQUITY LINE OF CREDIT (HELOC)

A HELOC is a line of credit secured by property, so lower rates can be offered compared to a standard, unsecured line of credit. Unlike a mortgage, the funds don't have to be advanced at closing. Payments are interest only and are charged only on funds advanced. The interest rate is usually the lender's prime rate plus (+) a premium. Current regulations limit the HELOC portion of a mortgage to 65% of the property's value.

BENCHMARK RATE

The benchmark rate is the posted rate for five-year fixed mortgages published by the Bank of Canada every Thursday. In determining this rate, the Bank of Canada surveys the posted rates of the six major banks and uses the mode (the most commonly posted rate). All insured borrowers, those with less than 20% down payment, must now "qualify" at the greater of the **contract rate** or the benchmark rate as a "stress test" to manage potential future increasing rates. Conventional borrowers as of January 1, 2018, need to qualify at the higher of the benchmark rate or 2% higher than the contract rate.

CONTRACT RATE

The interest rate the borrower commits to paying on the mortgage. For monoline lenders, the contract rate is their regular rate. For banks, the contract rate is usually a rate that is discounted below their "posted" or advertised rates. Bankers may refer to the contract rate as their "discounted rate."

REFINANCE

A mortgage process to access equity from one's property. The most common reasons for a refinance are to: take advantage of better interest rates and products, consolidate debts at a lower interest rate, complete renovations or purchase additional real estate.

SOLICITOR

An advisor, lawyer or notary who completes the legal requirements of the mortgage.

CHAPTER 5
Make the Present Count

Now we're going to transition from looking at credit and income history, our past, to what is happening in the present, the factors in the mortgage process where borrowers have a bit more control and decision-making opportunities.

How much do you have to invest? How much do you want to invest? What are your limitations and opportunities based on current rules and guidelines? What are the terms, product options and rates that are going to best suit your investment plans? What lenders have the product features that meet your needs and lifestyle?

What you decide today will have a significant impact on your overall return on investment. These few pages can help to explore your options so you have a better idea of what will be best suited to you.

THE PRESENT
Your Down Payment

In Canada, you can buy a home with a minimum down payment of 5% of the purchase price if you meet the insurer guidelines (insurers are: Canada Mortgage and Housing Corporation (CMHC), Genworth or Canada Guaranty).

PRESENT

- Down payment
- Product and rate

With an insured mortgage, the borrower pays a mortgage insurance premium. It can be paid up front but is most commonly wrapped into and amortized with the mortgage. More details on mortgage insurers and the cost of the premiums are covered in Chapter 11.

The insurance, or security, the government provides protects the lender's investment if the borrower defaults on the loan. For that reason, insured mortgages are more attractive to lenders, so they typically offer lower interest rates. You could argue that it's a win-win-win scenario: the homebuyer wins by being able to buy without the traditional 20% down payment requirement, the lender wins by having a loan secured by both the property and the government, and the government wins by collecting premiums from Canadians who rarely default. According to CMHC stats, Canada's mortgage delinquency rate is at the lowest level in decades, 0.25%.

DOWN PAYMENT RULES
The minimum down payment requirements are 5% for owner-occupied units for purchases under $500,000. In 2016, the federal government introduced new rules increasing the down payment minimum from 5% to 10% for a mortgage amount between $500,000 to $1 million.

For example, if a home is purchased for $800,000, the $40,000 (5%) down payment formerly required is now $55,000 (6.9%).

The Math

Before	After
$800,000 x 5%	($500,000 x 5%) + ($300,000 x 10%)
= $40,000	= $25,000 + $30,000
	= $55,000

81

In July 2012, there was a cap placed on insured mortgage property values. Properties over $1 million can no longer be insured, so homebuyers must have a down payment of at least 20% on purchases of homes over $1 million. Investment and rental properties also require a minimum down payment of 20%.

Non-resident files typically require a minimum 35% investment. The standard for bare land is a 50% down payment. In both these cases, there can be some exceptions to the rules.

New builds will depend on the builder and the contract. Some may require as little as 5% down while others may require separate instalments at certain milestones that could total 25% or possibly more for a down payment.

Construction loans also have a unique set-up, consisting of draws of mortgage funds rather than a lump-sum mortgage. The borrower needs to have funds available upfront to get the project going. I usually recommend clients have at least 40% of the build cost available, or more if the land is not yet owned. A lender may advance up to 65% to purchase the land initially, with the second advance accessible when the build is ~40% complete, that is, the roof on and the building weather protected. Once the project is complete, the borrower can apply for a standard mortgage on the property to get the invested capital back. However, until then, the borrower must carry a large portion of the initial costs.

In BC, the provincial government introduced a program, the BC Home Owner Mortgage and Equity Partnership (HOME) Program, available from January 2017 to March 2020, to help first-time homebuyers purchase with as little as 2.5% down. (Find more about this program on page 186.)

The BC HOME Partnership program, along with other cost-saving programs found in Chapter 10, provides opportunities to buy without having to save for decades. Getting on the property ladder can be done with some pig-headed discipline and a smart saving plan. Enlisting parental support can also help if it's available.

DOWN PAYMENT SOURCES

The down payment can come from a variety of sources: savings, stocks, investments, RRSPs, gifted funds from immediate family, the BC HOME Partnership, equity from a property you own or even borrowed funds. Over the required minimum, it is up to you to decide on the amount and sources.

Yes, you need access to money to fund your down payment, but you do have options and some control.

The amount of the down payment and the source of the funds could impact the mortgage approval amount. Some lenders have restrictions on down payment sources they allow depending on the property type or use. For example, most lenders don't allow rental properties to use gifted funds for the down payment. Otherwise, for the most part, almost any source is fine if it can be verified through documentation.

The documentation is not only required to meet the lender's guidelines. The government also enforces a minimum standard in accordance with the Financial Transactions and Reports Analysis Centre of Canada (FINTRAC) in support of anti-money laundering initiatives and provisions.

Most lenders require a complete 90-day history showing the down payment source. If the loan is conventional, there are options for 30-day verification. If there are any sizeable cash transfers into or out of the accounts provided, the lender will ask for documentation showing the source or destination of those funds, per FINTRAC's standards. If you're interested, more details on FINTRAC are available at its website, *www.fintrac-canafe.gc.ca.*

DEPOSIT VS. DOWN PAYMENT

The deposit is different than the down payment. Your deposit amount will eventually go towards your total down payment; however, the deposit is required immediately, usually within 24 hours of subject removal. In subject-free offers, the deposit may be present along with the offer.

The down payment (minus your deposit amount) isn't required until just before or on your closing date.

DOWN PAYMENT DOCUMENTS

The types of down payment documents are noted in this chart, followed by samples of each type.

DOWN PAYMENT DOCUMENT REQUIREMENTS
Purchase, Refinance, Switch/Transfer

DOWN PAYMENT DOCUMENTATION	NOTES
90-day Account Statements	If money is coming from savings/investments/RRSPs, account statements must show: • Current balance • Borrower's name • Address, and • Account number
Gift Letter	If gifted funds are given from an immediate family member: • A lender-specific gift letter will be issued to sign by applicant and giftor(s). • Confirmation of gifted funds deposited into borrower's account must be provided. The deposit amount should match *exactly* the amount written on the gift letter. • If gift funds are considered large, the lender may ask to see the source of funds from the giftor's account.
Contact of Purchase & Sale	If a property has been sold
Statement of Adjustments	If a property has been sold
Closing Costs	A lender may also request to see that the borrower has access to an additional 1.5% of the purchase price to cover closing costs, such as property transfer tax and legal fees.

SAMPLE: DOWN PAYMENT DOCUMENT
Mortgage Statement

85

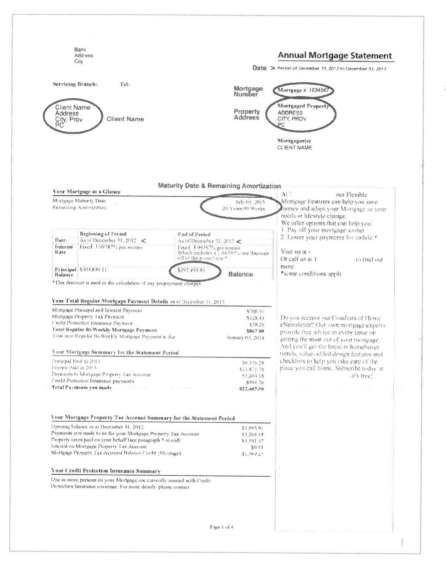

SAMPLE: DOWN PAYMENT DOCUMENT
Contract of Purchase and Sale

REAL ESTATE BOARD
OF GREATER VANCOUVER

PAGE 1 of _____ PAGES

CONTRACT OF PURCHASE AND SALE

86

PREPARED BY: _____ DATE: _____
(AGENCY - PLEASE PRINT)
ADDRESS: _____ PC: _____ PHONE: _____
PER: _____ MLS® No.: _____

SELLER:	BUYER:
SELLER:	BUYER:
ADDRESS:	ADDRESS:
PC:	PC:
PHONE:	PHONE:
RESIDENT OF CANADA ☐ NON-RESIDENT OF CANADA ☐	OCCUPATION:
as defined under the *Income Tax Act.*	

PROPERTY: Address: _____ Municipality: _____ PC: _____
Legal Description: _____
_____ (Property) PID # _____

The Buyer agrees to purchase the Property from the Seller on the following terms and subject to the following conditions:

1. **PURCHASE PRICE:** The purchase price of the Property will be _____
_____
_____ DOLLARS $_____ (Purchase Price)

2. **DEPOSIT:** A deposit of $_____ which will form part of the Purchase Price, will be paid on the following terms:
_____

All monies paid pursuant to this section (Deposit) will be delivered in trust to _____
and held in trust in accordance with the provisions of the *Real Estate Act.* In the event the Buyer fails to pay the Deposit as required by this Contract, the Seller may, at the Seller's option, terminate this Contract. The party who receives the Deposit is authorized to pay all or any portion of the Deposit to the Buyer's or Seller's conveyancer (the "Conveyancer") without further written direction of the Buyer or Seller, provided that: (a) the Conveyancer is a Lawyer or Notary; (b) such money is to be held in trust by the Conveyancer as stakeholder pursuant to the provisions of the *Real Estate Act* pending the completion of the transaction and not on behalf of any of the principals to the transaction; and (c) if the sale does not complete, the money should be returned to such party as stakeholder or paid into Court.

3. **TERMS AND CONDITIONS:** The purchase and sale of the Property includes the following terms and is subject to the following conditions: _____
_____
_____
_____

Each condition, if so indicated, is for the sole benefit of the party indicated. Unless each condition is waived or declared fulfilled by written notice given by the benefiting party to the other party on or before the date specified for each condition, this Contract will be terminated thereupon and the Deposit returnable in accordance with the *Real Estate Act.*

4. **COMPLETION:** The sale will be completed on _____ yr. _____ (Completion Date) at the appropriate Land Title Office.

5. **POSSESSION:** The Buyer will have vacant possession of the Property at 12 noon on _____ yr. _____ (Possession Date) OR, subject to the following existing tenancies, if any: _____

INITIALS

A035 - REV DEC/03

SAMPLE: DOWN PAYMENT DOCUMENT
Statement of Adjustment

LAWYERS

Head Office:

PURCHASERS' STATEMENT OF ADJUSTMENTS

Vendor:
Purchaser:
Civic:
Legal:
File Ref. No:
Completion Date: October 16, 2017   Adjustment Date: October 17, 2017   Possession Date: October 17, 2017

	DEBIT	CREDIT
Purchase Price	$444,000.00	
Property Transfer Tax	$0.00	
Deposit paid to Re/Max		$22,000.00
Balance of Mortgage Proceeds from The Bank of Nova Scotia		$355,100.00
Hub International Insurance Brokers - Insurance Binder	$75.00	
City of Vancouver - Property Tax Certificate	$67.33	
Strataco Management Ltd. - Strata Information	$57.75	
Stewart Title Guaranty Company - Title Insurance	$150.00	
Purchaser's portion of 2017 Property Taxes		
$975.71 - $845.00 (HOG) = $130.71		
$130.71 x 76/365 days	$27.22	
Purchaser's portion of Strata Maintenance Fees paid by Vendor		
$300.71 x 15/31 days	$145.50	
Law Society Trust Administration Fee	$15.75	
Credit from Irene Strong towards legal fees		$100.00
Credit to Seller for Tax Account Balance	$996.11	
Payment of Account :		
Fees		
Referral Discount	$916.16	
Taxable Disbursements	($100.00)	
Non-Taxable Disbursements	$75.00	
GST (5.00% x 891.16)	$208.84	
PST (7.00% x 816.16)	$44.56	
Total Account	$57.13	
	$1,201.69	
Sub Totals	$446,736.35	$377,200.00
Funds required from the Purchaser to complete should be direct deposited to the trust account of Lawyers In Trust. Please contact your legal assistant for account information.		$69,536.35
TOTALS	$446,736.35	$446,736.35

SAMPLE: DOWN PAYMENT DOCUMENT
Account/Investment/RRSP Statement

my statement

Account number: 123456789

Account Number

Name

Client Name
Address
City, Prov PC

For more information

Sign on to

Call

For the period January 1 to March 31, 2014   **3 Month History**

How the value of my plans changed this period

Value of my plans on January 1, 2014	$33,143.60
My contributions	$3,074.03
My employer's contributions	$3,058.22
Fees	-$43.07
Dividends	$65.62
My investment gains and losses	$3,189.61
Value of my plans on March 31, 2014	**$42,488.01**

What's inside

Details of my plans	2
Information I should know	5
Glossary of terms	5

Personal rates of return for my plans

3 MONTH	YEAR-TO-DATE	1 YEAR	3 YEAR	5 YEAR	SINCE JUNE 1, 2012
8.9%	8.9%	20.6%	-	-	22.5%

Your personal rates of return are net of management fees. For information on how we calculate your personal rates of return, please see the glossary on page 5 or sign in to your account at

My plans and their values

Hourly EEs BC & Yukon Pension Plan	$28,411.62
Employee Share Purchase Plan-Registered	$14,076.39
Value of my plans on March 31, 2014	**$42,488.01**

SAMPLE: DOWN PAYMENT DOCUMENT
Gift Letter

Gift Letter

Date: _____

To Whom It May Concern:

This letter confirms the undersigned is making a gift of $_____ to:

_____
(print names of recipients)

For use toward the purchase of the property located at:

_____
(address of the property being mortgaged)

We the undersigned, Recipients and Donors, hereby certify that:
1) No part of this gift is being provided by a third party having any interest (direct or indirect) in the sale of the subject property;
2) The money is a genuine gift and does not have to be repaid; and
3) The donor is an immediate family member

Recipients

Name: _____   Name: _____

Signature: _____   Signature: _____

Date: _____   Date: _____

Donors

Name: _____   Name: _____

Relationship: _____   Relationship: _____

Signature: _____   Signature: _____

Date: _____   Date: _____

Address: _____

Telephone: _____

Verification of Gift Source (needed only if Donor is in possession of funds)
Choose one of the options below to verify sufficient assets to cover the amount of the gift.
1) Bring this form to your bank/trust company and have them fill out the bottom of this form; or
2) Attach copies of bank or investment statements showing funds are available for the amount being given.

Bank/Trust Company Name/Address (stamped):

_____
Signature of Representative

_____
Date

THE PRESENT
Choosing a Mortgage Product and Rate

Although the lenders dictate rates, you have the choice on the type of product, options and features. You choose from those available to you, whether you are purchasing, **refinancing**, completing an **equity take-out**, **porting** your mortgage, **switching** to a new lender or leveraging your equity through a **reverse mortgage**.

PRESENT

- Down payment
- Product and rate

Mortgages can be in **first**, **second** or **third** position and they can come in a multitude of options: **closed** or **open**; fixed or variable; six-month or one-, two-, three-, four-, five-, six-, seven- or 10-year terms. They can be insured or uninsured; have unique features like the all-in-ones and home equity line of credit; and you can select from low frills (i.e., limited mortgage features) or full frills (i.e., extensive mortgage features)—it's up to you to decide.

That said, the type of mortgage product you choose may impact how much you qualify to borrow.

These are the key points to consider when selecting products and rates:

TERM

The term you choose will depend largely on what your short- and possibly long-term plans are. Lenders usually have six-month, one-year, two-year, three-year, four-year, five-year, six-year, seven-year, and ten-year fixed terms. Variable is mostly available as a five-year term with some lenders offering a three-year option.

Traditionally, six-month and one-year terms are some of the highest rates along with the six-, seven-, and 10-year terms. Two-year would be the lowest, with incremental increases up to the five-year.

Since closed mortgages come with prepayment penalties, selecting a term should be an important consideration, especially if you have any possibility of selling or refinancing within your term.

LINGO!

REFINANCE

(Also Referred to as Debt Restructuring)

A mortgage process to access equity from one's property. The most common reasons for a refinance are to: take advantage of better interest rates and products, consolidate debts at a lower interest rate, complete renovations or purchase additional real estate.

EQUITY TAKE-OUT (ETO)

An equity take-out mortgage can be accessed through a full refinance, a second mortgage or a home equity line of credit. It provides the borrower with access to the home's equity in cash for common needs such as debt consolidation, investments, down payments and projects such as renovations. Some lenders have a maximum ETO limit.

PORTABLE MORTGAGE

Portability allows the transfer of a mortgage to another home with little or no penalty when the existing home sells. Mortgage default insurance can also be ported to the new home. Both the mortgage and insurance products will have a restricted time allowable for porting.

To port a mortgage, you must requalify for the mortgage amount you are asking for. Different lender products will have different porting timelines. Most will allow 30 to 90 days to complete a port. Low-frills products usually have restrictive use or no portability options.

SWITCH/TRANSFER

At renewal, it may make sense to change lenders, either for a better rate or a better product. A switch/transfer program allows a borrower to move a current mortgage "as is" (same amount and amortization) to a new lender. The lender will usually cover legal and discharge fees as an extra incentive to move.

REVERSE MORTGAGE

A reverse mortgage is a loan secured against the value of your home. Unlike a loan or a regular mortgage, with a reverse mortgage you are not required to make payments. You only repay the loan when you move or sell your home.

This is a specialty product designed mainly for retired or retiring people. It's an option to consider if income levels are too low to service a standard mortgage and there is considerable equity in the property. This gives seniors the option to live at home, without having to feel forced to move and leave their community or downgrade their lifestyle. The interest rates on reverse mortgages are higher than those on standard mortgages.

FIRST MORTGAGE

A first lien position on the property title that secures the mortgage. A first mortgage has priority over all other liens or claims on a property in the event of default. In other words, the lender with the first lien receives its money back before any other lenders or liens can receive payment.

SECOND & THIRD MORTGAGES

A lien on a property which is positioned behind the first mortgage. Due to the subordinate position, second and third mortgages are riskier, so they can come with higher interest rates and are typically offered for shorter terms.

CLOSED MORTGAGE

With a closed mortgage come rates that are lower than the open mortgage alternative. This has made closed mortgages the more popular option in the market. With a closed product there is limited (or possibly no) ability to repay the loan early, in full or in part, without prepayment penalties. Prepayment privileges allow smaller lump-sum payments or payment increases without penalty.

93

OPEN MORTGAGE

Borrowers can pay their mortgage in full or in part, at any time, without penalty.

Lenders charge higher interest rates on open mortgages to compensate them for the costs and risks of possibly having to re-lend the funds in a different interest rate environment. Therefore, open mortgages are the best option only when funds are required for very short terms, such as when you're refinancing and the closing date with the new lender extends past the maturity date of the original mortgage. If your funding needs extend beyond six months, it may be better to consider a variable-rate mortgage with three months' interest penalty costs.

FIXED VS. VARIABLE (FLOATING) RATE

Fixed-term mortgages, as implied in their name, maintain a constant interest rate for the **term**, providing payment predictability from month to month.

Variable-rate mortgages can fluctuate over their terms. There are two types, adjustable-rate mortgages (ARM) and variable-interest-rate mortgages (VRM or VIRM).

The ARM is the more common of the two; the interest rate and monthly payments are adjusted based on changes to the lender's prime rate. Adjustments to the payment are made so that the amortization period—the length of time required to pay the mortgage off at the current **payment schedule**—remains the same throughout the term.

LINGO!

TERM

The length of time the mortgage contract is in place. Terms can be open or closed and are usually for six months up to 10 years for fixed, and three and five years for variable.

FIXED-RATE MORTGAGE

The interest rate stays constant for the term of the mortgage.

Fixed rates give a borrower certainty about their mortgage payment. For the selected term, the borrower knows the interest rate and therefore the amount of the payments, through to the end of the term.

Prepayment penalties are usually the higher of the interest rate differential (IRD) calculation or three months interest.

VARIABLE-RATE MORTGAGE

"Variable" is the common term used for floating-interest-rate products. A lender's variable rate is based on its prime rate minus (–) a discount or plus (+) a premium.

There are two variable mortgage products, adjustable-rate mortgages (ARM) and variable-interest-rate mortgages (VRM or VIRM).

Adjustable-Rate Mortgage (ARM)

A mortgage where the interest rate and the monthly payments vary based on changes in market rates. Adjustments to the payment are made if the lender's prime rate changes. The amortization remains the same throughout the term.

Variable-Rate Mortgage (VRM or VIRM)

A mortgage for which the interest rate fluctuates with market rates. The payments will remain the same if there is movement in the lender's prime rate. The amortization period will adjust—longer or shorter—accordingly.

Penalties are usually limited to three months of interest, and there is no interest rate differential (IRD) calculation.

PAYMENT SCHEDULE

Borrowers can select the type of payment schedule they would like for their mortgage. The amount of the payment is determined by the mortgage amount, interest rate and amortization. It can be paid monthly, semi-monthly, biweekly, biweekly accelerated, weekly or weekly accelerated.

The accelerated payment options allow a borrower to make one additional monthly payment a year, effectively lowering the overall remaining amortization by approximately two to 3.5 years over a five-year term.

With VRMs, only the interest rate adjusts over the term. The payment remains the same, so the amortization period increases or decreases, depending on the adjustment made to the lender's prime rate.

Variable products give borrowers the option to "lock in"—to move from a floating (variable) rate to a fixed rate at any time, without penalty—when the new term is equal to or longer than the term remaining on the original mortgage. Some lenders offer other options as well.

Variable mortgages have historically translated into significant interest savings over the life of the mortgage. However, you must feel emotionally comfortable with the unpredictability of rate fluctuations and, with the ARM product, have the cash flow flexibility to make higher payments.

Different key drivers influence fixed and variable rates. The primary rate driver of fixed mortgages is the rates of Canadian government bonds; the primary rate driver of variable mortgages is the Bank of Canada's overnight rate.

How Fixed-Rate Mortgages are Set

Many things can affect fixed mortgage rates; however, the strongest correlation is to government bond yields. When bond yields increase mortgage rates will usually increase and vice versa. This is mostly because mortgage interest rates and government bonds are competing for the same investor. The pricing spread between the "safe" government five-year bond yields and the "more risky" five-year fixed mortgage rates varies depending on factors of competition in the mortgage market and the overall economy.

The graph below provides a 10-year history of the movement of Canadian bond yields and the mortgage discounted rates and mortgage posted rates.

COMPARISON OF CANADIAN BOND YIELD VS. MORTGAGE RATES DECEMBER 2007 TO AUGUST 2017

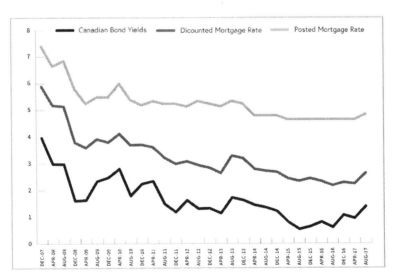

How Variable Mortgage Rates are Set

The overnight rate is set by the Bank of Canada, which maintains the country's monetary policy and inflation targets. Many factors influence the economy and inflation, such as unemployment, exports and manufacturing. There are eight overnight rate announcements each year.

The bank's overnight lending rate and monetary policy are the primary tools it uses to stimulate growth or contain inflation. It is also the rate at which major financial institutions borrow and lend one-day loans to each other.

Generally speaking, when inflation is rising, the Bank of Canada will increase the overnight rate to make borrowing money more expensive, which helps to slow a rapidly growing economy.

Conversely, when inflation is low, the Bank of Canada will decrease the overnight rate to improve the attractiveness of borrowing and stimulate the economy. Lenders' prime rates correlate with the overnight rate. When the overnight rate increases, lenders' prime rates increase, which in turn increases the variable rates lenders charge borrowers. Variable mortgages are set up as prime (+) plus (a bonus) or prime (–) minus (a discount).

Example: You complete a mortgage with a variable rate of prime–0.6%. The lender's current prime rate is 3.2%, so your rate is currently 2.6%. If the overnight rate increases by 0.25%, it is likely that the lender will increase its prime rate by 0.25%, to 3.45%. Your rate will now be 2.85%, and if you are in an ARM product, your payments will go up accordingly.

Overall, when interest rates are low and are not expected to fall further, it is typically advisable to lock in, as variables rates will stay the same or increase.

On the other hand, if you expect interest rates to fall, then a variable rate is attractive, as you will be able to benefit from the lower interest rate expected ahead.

Similarly, if the spread between the variable rate and the fixed rate is significant, it may not be worth paying the premium for the stability protection of a fixed rate.

For your review, the following chart is a historical look at the changes to the overnight rate target and how it impacted a lender's prime rate.

BANK OF CANADA OVERNIGHT RATE:
Announcements Impacting Change to Prime

DATE	OVERNIGHT RATE	PRIME RATE OF A MAJOR BANK LENDER	% DIFFERENCE
May 2006 - Jul 2007	4.25%	6.00%	1.75%
Jul 2007 - Dec 2007	4.50%	6.25%	1.75%
Dec 2007 - Jan 2008	4.25%	6.00%	1.75%
Jan 2008 - Mar 2008	4.00%	5.75%	1.75%
Mar 2008 - Apr 2008	3.50%	5.25%	1.75%
Apr 2008 - Oct 2008	3.00%	4.75%	1.75%
Oct 2008	2.50%	4.50%	2.00%
Oct 2008 - Dec 2008	2.25%	4.00%	1.75%
Dec 2008 - Jan 2009	1.50%	3.50%	2.00%
Jan 2009 - Mar 2009	1.00%	3.00%	2.00%
Mar 2009 - Apr 2009	0.50%	2.50%	2.00%
Apr 2009 - Jun 2010	0.25%	2.25%	2.00%
Jun 2010 - Jul 2010	0.50%	2.50%	2.00%
Jul 2010 - Sep 2010	0.75%	2.75%	2.00%
Sep 2010 - Jan 2015	1.00%	3.00%	2.00%
Jan 2015 - Jul 2015	0.75%	2.85%	2.10%
Jul 2015 - Jul 2017	0.50%	2.70%	2.20%
Jul 2017 - Sep 2017	0.75%	2.95%	2.20%
Sep 2017 - Jan 2018	1.00%	3.20%	2.20%
Jan 2018	1.25%	3.45%	2.20%

INSURABILITY

Insured

Mortgage regulation changes in 2016 required all insured borrowers, those with a down payment of less than 20%, to qualify at the benchmark rate. The maximum amortization for insured products is 25 years. These borrowers benefit from the best rates on the market as they come with government-secured backing.

Insurable

Conventional borrowers—those with a down payment of 20% or greater—can access lower rates if they are "insurable," meaning they meet the qualifying "stress test" rate, the amortization is no more than 25 years and the property value is under $1 million. Multiple rentals with two to four units can be insured if they meet these requirements.

Uninsurable

Conventional borrowers—those with a down payment of 20% or greater—who may have one or more of the stipulations on their mortgage:

- an amortization greater than 25 years,
- the purchase price is over $1 million,
- they are completing a refinance,
- they are purchasing a single rental unit, and/or
- they are qualifying at the contract rate, if available.

With reduced competition in the market for these borrowers and higher product costs, uninsurable mortgages typically have higher interest rates than the insured or insurable products.

ALL-IN-ONES AND HELOCS

All-in-one products (mortgage debt and income are collected in the same account) and HELOCs can add a level of flexibility should a borrower need early prepayment or to access available equity at a time of low funds. They are particularly effective for small business owners or those with irregular income. They have the potential to provide a level of security as well as decrease the overall interest costs if income outpaces the debt.

PRODUCT FEATURES

The mortgage products known as "full frills" have all the bells and whistles the lender offers, which can include options for prepayment, the ability to move (port) the mortgage to a new home or have your mortgage assumed by a qualified buyer of your home (**assumable mortgage**).

Those known as "low frills," on the other hand, have limitations. Borrowers are offered a lower rate with restrictions. There may be no prepayment options, they may not be able to prepay their mortgage unless they sell their home (called a **bona-fide sales clause**), or they may only be able to refinance with the same lender. These products can be very limiting and end up costing much more than the borrower saved in interest costs. It is very important to proceed with caution on these options as they are suited only to a small part of the population.

LINGO!

ASSUMABLE MORTGAGE

An assumable mortgage is a type of financing arrangement in which the outstanding mortgage and its terms can be transferred from the current owner to a buyer.

This is a product option that would be desirable if rates started to increase and a buyer might be more enticed to purchase a property if they could also assume a lower interest rate from the seller for the mortgage they would need to purchase the home.

BONA-FIDE SALES CLAUSE

The borrower is only able to pay off the mortgage mid-term if the property is sold to a third party.

This is a clause that is more commonly found in mortgage products offering lower-than-usual market rates. This is a dangerous clause as there is no option to refinance, which could be costly to the homeowner and not worth the initial interest savings the product provided.

101

PREPAYMENT PRIVILEGE OPTIONS

Most mortgage products offer prepayment options, which entitle a borrower to put more funds toward the mortgage without penalty. The options range from lender to lender, but the standard is for a borrower to be able to increase mortgage payments by 10% to 25% (in some cases up to 100%) each year or pay off 10% to 25% of the original mortgage amount as a lump sum annually. How this can be done ranges from lender to lender as well. Some limit the payment increases and lump-sum payments to once each year, on the mortgage anniversary date, with a minimum of $1,000, while other lenders allow prepayments on any payment date with a minimum of $100. Other lenders offer double-up, match-a-payment, skip-a-payment or other exclusive branded options.

PREPAYMENT PENALTIES

Statistically speaking, a borrower has a 60% chance of breaking a five-year mortgage by month 38, just over three years. Breaking a mortgage before the end of its term can come with some costly penalties, especially if you are in a fixed mortgage. Therefore, potential penalty costs should be a factor in deciding what product is right for you now.

Fixed mortgage penalties are typically the higher of the equivalent of three months' interest or the **interest rate differential (IRD)**. Variable mortgage penalties are typically limited to three-months' interest. A rule of thumb is that the IRD calculation will be approximately 4.5% of the outstanding mortgage balance. The three-months' interest is about 0.5%. A calculation example is provided for you in the coming pages.

Monoline lenders and banks differ in many ways, but a significant difference for borrowers is their interest rates. Banks have two rates: their posted rates and their discounted rates. Posted rates are publicly advertised rates, which are typically much higher than the current best market rates. Banks discount posted rates to be competitive, which Scotiabank and TD offer through the **broker channel**.

The posted rate is a money generator for the banks. A couple of ways it can translate into higher profits include:

Renewals: A bank will usually send a renewal notice with its posted rates. If you sign without further negotiation, you can be locked into a new term at rates as much as 2% higher than the current market rates.

IRD calculations: Banks use an IRD calculation of their posted rate minus the discount given. This can mean much higher IRD penalty costs.

LINGO!

INTEREST RATE DIFFERENTIAL (IRD)

If you pay off your mortgage before your term matures, you will likely have to pay penalties to compensate the lender for the contract breach.

Today, most closed, fixed-rate mortgages have a prepayment penalty that is three months' interest or the IRD—whichever is higher.

Most variable-rate mortgage contracts include only a three-months' interest penalty.

The IRD calculation can be drastically different from one lender to another, specifically between a bank and a monoline lender. For this reason and others, it is important to look at all the aspects of the mortgage product and not just the current rate being offered by the lender.

BROKER CHANNEL

The two primary ways to arrange a mortgage are to go directly to a bank or credit union or to engage a mortgage broker who represents many lenders and can advise you and negotiate on your behalf. Not all major banks offer mortgages through mortgage brokers. The "broker channel" refers to those lenders who lend to homeowners, in whole or in part, through brokers.

IRD Calculation: Bank vs. Monoline

Let's assume two borrowers complete mortgages for the same amount. Borrower A finances through a bank and borrower B finances through a monoline lender.

They are offered the same five-year mortgage rate, 2.69%. The difference is that borrower A's rate is based on the bank's posted five-year rate (4.64%) minus their current discount of 1.95%, for a discounted rate of 2.69%. Borrower B's rate is the monoline lender's standard 2.69%.

Three years later, both borrowers sell their property and need to pay out their remaining mortgage balance of $300,000 early. Two years remain on their commitment.

The following are the respective penalty calculations, assuming the current two-year rates are 2.39% for the monoline lender (the bank's discounted rate) and 3.09% for the bank's posted rate.

Three months' interest penalty calculations:

$$= \frac{\text{Interest rate x mortgage balance} \quad \text{x} \quad 3 \text{ months}}{12 \text{ months}}$$

$$= \frac{2.69\% \text{ x } \$300,000 \quad \text{x} \quad 3 \text{ months}}{12}$$

= **$2,017.50**

Bank IRD calculation

(Interest rate – (remaining term posted rate – discount given)) x mortgage balance x years remaining

= (2.69% – (3.09% – 1.95%)) x $300,000 x 2 years
= (2.69% – 1.14%) x $300,000 x 2 years
= 1.55% x $300,000 x 2 years
= **$9,300**

Monoline IRD calculation

(Interest rate – remaining term current interest rate) x mortgage balance x years remaining

= (2.69% rate – 2.39%) x $300,000 x 2 years
= 0.3% x $300,000 x 2 years
= **$1,800**

Borrower A would have a **penalty of $9,300** through the bank because the IRD calculation is higher than the three months' interest.

Borrower B would have a **penalty of $2,017.50** through the monoline lender. The three months' interest penalty is higher than the IRD; therefore, the lender would charge the three-months' interest penalty.

Adding each of the borrower's penalty costs as part of the mortgage, the effective annual percentage rate (APR) paid by borrower A would have been approximately 3.66% and borrower B would be approximately 2.89%.

The importance of this example is not to say that banks are bad or malicious. They provide an excellent product selection with unique solutions that can be tailored to a client's needs. They are always a financing option to be considered.

I share this example to draw attention to the fact that not all mortgage products and interest rates are created equal. It's important to review and consider your short- and long-term plans. Plans can change, understandably. Knowing the product's benefits and limitations, such as penalty costs, can provide you with the greatest protection and flexibility over the entire term of your mortgage. And that can save you money and headaches.

Many lenders offer online prepayment calculators, including B2B Bank, First National, MCAP, Merix, Scotiabank and TD Canada Trust. *Google prepayment calculator and the bank's name* or just visit their websites and follow the links.

CHAPTER 6
Back to the Future, Mortgage Edition

You have navigated your way through the past, learning how to manage your credit and what you need to validate your income. You then walked through your present options with considerations for down payment, products and rates.

Finally, you are going to turn your sights towards the future. What do you want to own? What is the purpose of the property?

The last two factors a mortgage approval relies on are both tied to the property —what kind of property it is and how it will be used by the owner.

This section is not as extensive as the previous two, but it carries great weight in the lender's approval and has the potential to impact the requirements the borrower must meet for credit, income and down payment as well as limit the products and rate options available.

THE FUTURE
Property Type

While we tend to think of the residential real estate market as consisting of detached homes and condos that are purchased for investment purposes or as a primary home, there are many different types of property.

> **FUTURE**
>
> • Property type
> • Property use

They include:

- low-rise apartments,
- high-rise apartments,
- townhouses,
- duplexes,
- single-family dwellings,
- mixed-use (residential and commercial),
- vacation homes,
- agricultural land reserve (ALR) property,
- farms,
- cabins,
- mobile homes,
- construction and bare land, etc.

Not all lenders will consider all property types, but if it's what you want, it's usually possible to find a lender. It might not be at the best market rates or with the usual product options, so cost versus desire may come into play.

Ultimately, it's up to the buyer to decide what they wish to make an offer on and then it's up to the broker to find the best fit in terms of lender and product.

NOTE: Some of the more challenging properties to find lender interest include: co-ops; remediated grow-ops or drug labs; properties containing vermiculite or asbestos or with tube and knob or aluminum wiring; strata properties with pending assessments or with water damage or major leaks noted in their meeting minutes; age-restricted properties; self-managed strata units; mixed-use properties; hobby farms or land with livestock present; leasehold and crown land. The list could go on...

PROPERTY FACTORS
Ownership

Ownership may be **freehold**, **leasehold** or **strata**. Depending on the type of ownership, there will be more or less lender interest. For example, few lenders are willing to lend on leasehold properties.

Property Details

For the **subject property**, property taxes and heat must be included in the mortgage application. Depending on the property and area, these two factors can have an influence on a borrowers maximum borrowing power. Some lenders will allow the BC Home Owners Grant (HOG) to be removed from the tax amount, while others require the full amount to be included in the debt ratios. Most lenders have a general rule of $100 per month for heat for a single-family dwelling or townhouses and $50 for condo units, while other lenders calculate on a cost per square foot. Strata units must include the strata fees.

With the evolution of micro condos, it should also be noted that some lenders have a minimum square footage requirement; however, exceptions can be made.

If the property is a rental unit or has a basement suite or there are other **non-subject properties** owned by the borrower, each lender will account for rental income differently. This is one of the ways a broker can offer a huge advantage. The most common, and most conservative, is using 50% of the rental income and adding it back to the borrower's income, with 100% of the mortgage payments, property taxes and heat, as well as 50% of the strata fees, accounted in the debt service ratios. In the broker channel, there are lenders offering more progressive options for factoring rental income. An "offset" equation or the use of a rental worksheet has the potential to eliminate the negative liability of the rental property or even add a positive cash flow to the application.

LINGO!

FREEHOLD

A type of homeownership: full and exclusive ownership of property (house and land) for an indefinite period.

LEASEHOLD

A type of homeownership: full and exclusive ownership of property (house and land) for a defined period.

STRATA

A type of homeownership: owners own the unit they live in while they also share ownership of common areas such as parkades, hallways, elevators, lobbies, gyms, amenity rooms and landscaping with other owners in the building or complex.

SUBJECT PROPERTY

The property being purchased, refinanced or renewed.

NON-SUBJECT PROPERTY

Property added to the application in addition to the subject property (the one being purchasing, refinanced or renewed). A non-subject property is usually an investment property or a second home owned by the applicant.

PROPERTY DOCUMENTATION

Once the seller accepts your offer on a property, all property documents should be made available to the mortgage broker, if they were not provided earlier. The next chart provides a list of the common property documents required by lenders followed by their corresponding samples.

PROPERTY DOCUMENT REQUIREMENTS
Purchase, Refinance and Switch/Transfer

PROPERTY DOCUMENTATION	NOTES
Contract of Purchase and Sale & Subject Removal	Must be fully signed and include the subject removal date, closing date and list of subjects. Once subjects are removed, the signed subject removal will need to be provided to the lender.
MLS Listing	Needs to be produced by the seller's or buyer's agent including name and contact details.
Property Disclosure Statement (PDS)	A document a seller completes disclosing any known defects on the property. The document is for the buyers' protection. For rental units, it is common for the PDS to be crossed out entirely.
Strata Form B (Strata only)	Confirm strata fees, contingency fund and other important building aspects including strata financials.
Depreciation Report (Strata only)	The depreciation report among other things provides an overview of the expected maintenance costs and repairs an owner may be responsible for in the coming years.
Strata Documents (Strata only)	Additional documents may be requested by the lender for clarification. These can include: 1. 2 years AGM minutes 2. 1 year of strata meeting minutes 3. Engineer reports 4. Work completion certificates
Mortgage Statement	If refinance, equity take-out (ETO), or switch/transfer mortgage, a mortgage statement will be needed for each property owned.
Property Tax Notice(s)	If refinance, equity take-out (ETO), or switch/transfer mortgage, the property tax notice for each property will be requested.

SAMPLE: PROPERTY DOCUMENT
Contract of Purchase and Sale

112

REAL ESTATE BOARD
OF GREATER VANCOUVER

PAGE 1 of _____ PAGES

CONTRACT OF PURCHASE AND SALE

PREPARED BY: _____ DATE: _____
ADDRESS: _____ (AGENCY: PLEASE PRINT) _____ PC: _____ PHONE: _____
PER: _____ MLS® No.: _____

SELLER:	BUYER:
SELLER:	BUYER:
ADDRESS:	ADDRESS:
PC:	PC:
PHONE:	PHONE:
RESIDENT OF CANADA ☐ NON-RESIDENT OF CANADA ☐ as defined under the *Income Tax Act*.	OCCUPATION:

PROPERTY: Address: _____ Municipality: _____ PC: _____
Legal Description: _____
_____ (Property) PID # _____

The Buyer agrees to purchase the Property from the Seller on the following terms and subject to the following conditions:

1. **PURCHASE PRICE:** The purchase price of the Property will be _____
_____
_____ DOLLARS $ _____ (Purchase Price)

2. **DEPOSIT:** A deposit of $ _____ which will form part of the Purchase Price, will be paid on the following terms:
_____

All monies paid pursuant to this section (Deposit) will be delivered in trust to _____ and held in trust in accordance with the provisions of the *Real Estate Act*. In the event the Buyer fails to pay the Deposit as required by this Contract, the Seller may, at the Seller's option, terminate this Contract. The party who receives the Deposit is authorized to pay all or any portion of the Deposit to the Buyer's or Seller's conveyancer (the "Conveyancer") without further written direction of the Buyer or Seller, provided that: (a) the Conveyancer is a Lawyer or Notary; (b) such money is to be held in trust by the Conveyancer as stakeholder pursuant to the provisions of the *Real Estate Act* pending the completion of the transaction and not on behalf of any of the principals to the transaction; and (c) if the sale does not complete, the money should be returned to such party as stakeholder or paid into Court.

3. **TERMS AND CONDITIONS:** The purchase and sale of the Property includes the following terms and is subject to the following conditions: _____
_____
_____

Each condition, if so indicated, is for the sole benefit of the party indicated. Unless each condition is waived or declared fulfilled by written notice given by the benefiting party to the other party on or before the date specified for each condition, this Contract will be terminated thereupon and the Deposit returnable in accordance with the *Real Estate Act*.

4. **COMPLETION:** The sale will be completed on _____ yr _____ (Completion Date) at the appropriate Land Title Office.

5. **POSSESSION:** The Buyer will have vacant possession of the Property at 12 noon on _____ yr _____ (Possession Date) OR, subject to the following existing tenancies, if any: _____

INITIALS

A035 - REV. DEC/09

SAMPLE: PROPERTY DOCUMENT
MLS Listing

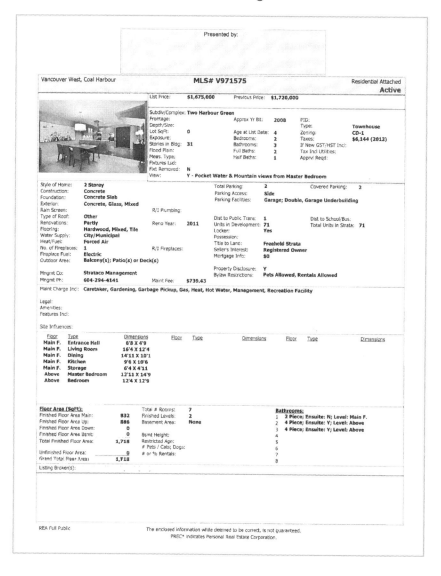

Presented by:

Vancouver West, Coal Harbour	**MLS# V971575**	Residential Attached
		Active

List Price: **$1,675,000**   Previous Price: **$1,720,000**

Subdiv/Complex: **Two Harbour Green**

Frontage:		Approx Yr Blt:	2008	PID:
Depth/Size:				Type:	**Townhouse**
Lot SqFt:	0	Age at List Date:	4	Zoning:	**CD-1**
Exposure:		Bedrooms:	2	Taxes:	**$6,144 (2012)**
Stories in Bldg:	31	Bathrooms:	3	If New GST/HST Incl:
Flood Plain:		Full Baths:	2	Tax Incl Utilities:
Meas. Type:		Half Baths:	1	Apprvl Reqd:
Fixtures Lsd:				
Fixt Removed:	N			
View:	Y - Pocket Water & Mountain views from Master Bedroom

Style of Home:	2 Storey		Total Parking:	2	Covered Parking:	2
Construction:	Concrete		Parking Access:	Side
Foundation:	Concrete Slab		Parking Facilities:	Garage; Double, Garage Underbuilding
Exterior:	Concrete, Glass, Mixed		
Rain Screen:		R/I Plumbing:	
Type of Roof:	Other		Dist to Public Trans:	1	Dist to School/Bus:
Renovations:	Partly		Units in Development:	71	Total Units in Strata: 71
Flooring:	Hardwood, Mixed, Tile	Reno Year: 2011	Locker:	Yes
Water Supply:	City/Municipal		Possession:
Heat/Fuel:	Forced Air		Title to Land:	Freehold Strata
No. of Fireplaces:	1	R/I Fireplaces:	Seller's Interest:	Registered Owner
Fireplace Fuel:	Electric		Mortgage Info:	$0
Outdoor Area:	Balcony(s); Patio(s) or Deck(s)		
			Property Disclosure:	Y
Mngmt Co:	Strataco Management		Bylaw Restrictions:	Pets Allowed, Rentals Allowed
Mngmt Ph:	604-294-4141	Maint Fee: $739.43	

Maint Charge Incl: Caretaker, Gardening, Garbage Pickup, Gas, Heat, Hot Water, Management, Recreation Facility

Legal:
Amenities:
Features Incl:

Site Influences:

Floor	Type	Dimensions	Floor	Type	Dimensions	Floor	Type	Dimensions
Main F.	Entrance Hall	6'8 X 4'9						
Main F.	Living Room	16'4 X 12'4						
Main F.	Dining	14'11 X 10'1						
Main F.	Kitchen	9'6 X 10'6						
Main F.	Storage	6'4 X 4'11						
Above	Master Bedroom	12'11 X 14'9						
Above	Bedroom	12'4 X 12'9						

Floor Area (SqFt):				Bathrooms:	
Finished Floor Area Main:	832	Total # Rooms:	7	1	2 Piece; Ensuite: N; Level: Main F.
Finished Floor Area Up:	886	Finished Levels:	2	2	4 Piece; Ensuite: Y; Level: Above
Finished Floor Area Down:	0	Basement Area:	None	3	4 Piece; Ensuite: Y; Level: Above
Finished Floor Area Bsmt:	0	Bsmt Height:		4	
Total Finished Floor Area:	1,718	Restricted Age:		5	
		# Pets / Cats; Dogs:		6	
Unfinished Floor Area:	0	# or % Rentals:		7	
Grand Total Floor Area:	1,718			8	

Listing Broker(s):

REA Full Public

The enclosed information while deemed to be correct, is not guaranteed.
PREC* indicates Personal Real Estate Corporation.

113

SAMPLE: PROPERTY DOCUMENT
Property Disclosure Statement

PROPERTY DISCLOSURE STATEMENT
RESIDENTIAL

PAGE 1 of _____ PAGES

Date of disclosure: _____

The following is a statement made by the seller concerning the premises or bare-land strata lot located at:

ADDRESS/BARE-LAND STRATA LOT #:   **(the "Premises")**

THE SELLER IS RESPONSIBLE for the accuracy of the answers on this property disclosure statement and where uncertain should reply "Do Not Know." This property disclosure statement constitutes a representation under any Contract of Purchase and Sale if so agreed, in writing, by the seller and the buyer

THE SELLER SHOULD INITIAL THE APPROPRIATE REPLIES.

1. LAND	YES	NO	DO NOT KNOW	DOES NOT APPLY
A. Are you aware of any encroachments, unregistered easements or unregistered rights-of-way?			X	X
B. Are you aware of any past or present underground oil storage tank(s) on the Premises?			X	X
C. Is there a survey certificate available?			X	X
D. Are you aware of any current or pending local improvement levies/charges?			X	X
E. Have you received any other notice or claim affecting the Premises from any person or public body?			X	X

2. SERVICES	YES	NO	DO NOT KNOW	DOES NOT APPLY
A. Indicate the water system(s) the Premises use: Municipal ⬜ Community ⬜ Private ⬜ Well ⬜ Not Connected ⬜ Other_____				
B. Are you aware of any problems with the water system?			X	
C. Are records available regarding the quantity and quality of the water available?				
D. Indicate the sanitary sewer system the Premises are connected to. Municipal ⬜ Community ⬜ Septic ⬜ Lagoon ⬜ Not Connected ⬜ Other_____				
E. Are you aware of any problems with the sanitary sewer system?			X	
F. Are there any current service contracts, (i.e., septic removal or maintenance)?			X	
G. If the system is septic or lagoon and installed after May 31, 2005, are maintenance records available?			X	

3. BUILDING	YES	NO	DO NOT KNOW	DOES NOT APPLY
A. To the best of your knowledge, are the exterior walls insulated?				
B. To the best of your knowledge, is the ceiling insulated?				
C. To the best of your knowledge, have the Premises ever contained any asbestos products?				
D. Has a final building inspection been approved or a final occupancy permit been obtained?				
E. Has the fireplace, fireplace insert, or wood stove installation been approved by local authorities?				
F. Are you aware of any infestation or unrepaired damage by insects or rodents?			X	X
G. Are you aware of any structural problems with any of the buildings?			X	X
H. Are you aware of any additions or alterations made in the last sixty days?			X	X
I. Are you aware of any additions or alterations made without a required permit and final inspection, e.g., building, electrical, gas, etc.?			X	X

INITIALS

SAMPLE: PROPERTY DOCUMENT
Strata Form B

FORM B

INFORMATION CERTIFICATE
(Section 59)

The Owners, Strata Plan   certify that the information contained in this certificate with respect to   is correct as of the date of this certificate.

(a) Monthly strata fees payable by the owner of the strata lot described above: $235.63.

(b) Any amount owing to the strata corporation by the owner of the strata lot described above (other than an amount paid into court, or to the strata corporation in trust under section 114 of the Strata Property Act)? No

(c) Are there any agreements under which the owner of the strata lot described above takes responsibility for expenses relating to alterations to the strata lot, the common property or the common assets? No

(d) Any amount that the owner of the strata lot described above is obligated to pay in the future for a special levy that has already been approved? No

(e) Any amount by which the expenses of the strata corporation for the current fiscal year are expected to exceed the expenses budgeted for the fiscal year? No

(f) Amount in the contingency reserve account minus any expenditure's which have already been approved but not yet taken from the fund: Current CRF is $194,401.47 as of February 2017.

(g) Are there any amendments to the bylaws that are not yet filed in the land title office? No

(h) Are there any resolutions passed by a 3/4 vote or unanimous vote that are required to be filed in the land title office but that have not yet been filed in the land title office? No

(i) Has notice been given for any resolutions, requiring a 3/4 vote or unanimous vote or dealing with an amendment to the bylaws, that have not yet been voted on? No

(j) Is the strata corporation part to any court proceedings or arbitration, and/or are there any judgments or orders against the strata corporation? No

(k) Have any notices or work orders been received by the strata corporation that remain outstanding for the strata lot, the common property or the common assets? No

(l) Number of strata lots in the strata plan that are rented: 5, to the best of our knowledge.

(m) Are there parking stall(s) allocated to the strata lot

☐ No ☒ Yes

(i) If yes, complete the following by checking the correct box(es) and indicating the parking stall(s) to which the checked box(es) apply

☐ Parking stall(s) number(s) _____ is/are part of the strata lot

☐ Parking stall(s) number(s) _____ is/are separate strata lot(s) or parts of strata lot   [strata lot number(s) if known for each parking stall that is a separate strata lot or part of a separate strata lot]

☐ Parking stall(s) number(s) _____ is/are limited common property

☒ Parking stall(s) number(s) 32 is/are common property

(ii) For each parking stall allocated to the strata lot that is common property, check the correct box and complete the required information.

☐ Parking stall(s) number(s) _____ is/are allocated with strata council approval *

☐ Parking stall(s) number(s) _____ is/are allocated with strata council approval and

SAMPLE: PROPERTY DOCUMENT
Strata Form B Cont'd

rented at $_____ per month*

*Note: the allocation of a parking stall that is common property may be limited as short term exclusive use subject to section 76 of the Strata Property Act, or otherwise and may therefore be subject to change in the future.

(n)   Are there any storage locker(s) allocated to the strata lot?

☐ No   ☒ Yes

(ii) If yes, complete the following by checking the correct box(es) and indicated the parking stall(s) to which the checked box(es) apply

☐ Storage locker(s)_____ is/are part of the strata lot

☐ Storage locker(s) number(s) _____ is/are separate strata lot(s) or parts of strata lot [strata lot lot number(s), if known for each locker that is a separate strata lot or part of a separate strata lot]

☐ Storage locker(s) number(s)_____ is/are limited common property

☒ Storage locker(s) number(s) 38 is/are common property

*Note: The allocation of a storage locker that is common property may be limited as short term exclusive use subject to section 76 of the Strata Property Act, or otherwise, and may therefore be subject to change in the future.

Required Attachments

In addition to attachments mentioned above, section 59(4) of the Strata Property Act requires that copies of the following must be attached to this Information certificate:

☐ The rules of the strata corporation;

☐ The current budget of the strata corporation;

☐ The owner developer's Rental Disclosure Statement under section 139, if any; and

☐ The most recent depreciation report, in any obtained by the strata corporation under section 94

Date: September ___7___, 2017

Note: The information contained in this form is based on the best knowledge of ; _____ at the time of completion _____ does not warrant or make representations regarding the accuracy of the information which has been provided in it by the strata corporation and shall not be liable to any person relying on this form.

END OF DOCUMENT

SAMPLE: PROPERTY DOCUMENT
Strata Form B Cont'd

APPROVED 2017/2018 OPERATING BUDGET

INCOME:		2017 Approved
	SPECIAL ASSESSMENT	
4010	RENTAL INCOME	
4020	MAINTENANCE FEES	$ 195,000.00
4090	MISCELLANEOUS INCOME	$ 1,860.00
4054	LAUNDRY INCOME	$ 8,000.00
4080	PARKING INCOME	$ -
4110	INTEREST INCOME	$ 300.00
	OPERATING INCOME	$ 205,160.00

EXPENSES:		
6010	ACCOUNTING & AUDIT	$ 420.00
6020	BANK CHARGES	$ 108.00
6030	HVAC CONTRACT	$ 1,800.00
6032	HVAC REPAIRS	$ 3,000.00
6050	MANAGEMENT FEES	$ 17,496.00
6060	MAINTENANCE-ELEVATOR	$ 3,360.00
6062	CARETAKER	$ 26,780.00
6063	MAINTENANCE-LANDSCAPING	$ 18,000.00
6064	MAINTENANCE-ELECTRICAL	$ 804.00
6068	MAINTENANCE-SNOW REMOVAL	$ 480.00
6070	MAINTENANCE-WINDOW CLEAN	$ 720.00
6072	MAINTENANCE-EXTERIOR	$ 25,000.00
6074	MAINTENANCE-PLUMBING	$ 9,600.00
6080	MISC. BLDG. MAINT. & SUPPLIES	$ 960.00
6090	OFFICE EXPENSE	$ 840.00
6140	TRASH REMOVAL	$ 10,800.00
	PEST CONTROL	$ 2,000.00
6150	SECURITY-ALARM	$ 700.00
6152	FIRE & LIFE SAFETY SYSTEMS	$ 2,160.00
6180	ENTERPHONE	$ 360.00
6210	INSURANCE	$ 20,160.00
6066	RENTAL-LAUNDRY MACHINES	$ 1,500.00
6410	UTILITIES-ELECTRICITY	$ 10,200.00
6420	UTILITIES-GAS	$ 22,560.00
6510	WATER & SEWER	$ 14,400.00
	SUB-TOTAL	$ 194,208.00
	CONTINGENCY	$ 10,952.00
	TOTAL EXPENSES	$ 205,160.00
	SURPLUS (DEFICIT)	$ -

Taxes are included in all categories save for insurance

SAMPLE: PROPERTY DOCUMENT
Property Tax Notice

VANTAX

SAMPLE: PROPERTY DOCUMENT
Mortgage Statement

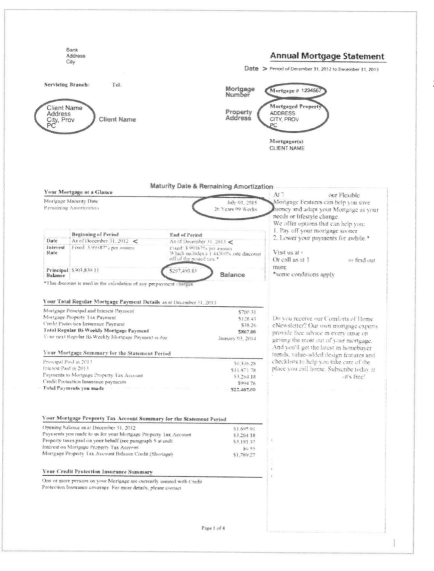

Page 1 of 4

INSURER'S APPROVAL

If the down payment is less than 20% of the purchase price, one of the mortgage insurance companies (CMHC, Genworth or Canada Guaranty) will have to approve the property in addition to the lender. If the lender has confirmed interest in the borrower and property, they will submit the file to the insurer for approval and confirmation of premium charges. For more on mortgage loan insurance and the insurers, see Chapter 11.

APPRAISAL

An appraisal of the property may be required to verify its value. If the insurer or lender cannot confirm an auto-valuation, it will request an appraisal as a condition of the approval. (Auto-valuations are provided by services that use mathematical modelling along with a sales database to provide a valuation without inspecting the property.) Appraisals are usually at the borrower's cost unless the property is insured, in which case the insurer covers the cost. Appraisals can range in price, depending on location and type of property, starting from about $250 in a standard metropolitan location to $800+ for a large acreage or remote area. The broker will order the appraisal because it must be completed by a lender-approved appraisal company and in some cases ordered through a third-party supplier (such as Solidifi, National Appraisal Services (NAS) or Real Property Solutions (RPS)).

What to expect with an appraisal

The appraisal company or a third-party supplier will contact you to arrange for payment by phone or email before an appointment can be arranged. Pay promptly: any delay can delay your mortgage approval, which can mean your financing won't be approved in time for **subject removal**.

The appraiser will then contact the listing agent (for a purchase) or the owner (for a refinance) to arrange for the appointment. At the appointment, the appraiser will usually take 10 to 20 minutes to view the interior and exterior area of the property. They will take pictures and take some notes on the home.

The appraiser will then generate a detailed report, specific to the lender's requirements, which gives a review of the property and provides recent comparable sales in the area to determine a market value estimate. These reports cannot be provided to the borrower.

In busy markets, appraisals can take some time, which should be considered when determining a subject removal date.

121

LINGO!

SUBJECT REMOVAL DATE

Except in the most competitive of markets, purchase offers are usually made subject to certain conditions, such as the satisfactory completion of a home inspection and financing arrangements. The potential buyer has until the subject removal date to remove these conditions. If financing is not arranged by this date, for example, the seller may agree to extend the date or may choose to "void" the offer in order to accept an offer from another potential buyer.

For a buyer to remove the financing subject, their lender must approve the income, down payment and property documents on or before the subject removal date.

THE FUTURE
Property Use

The use of your property also factors into the minimum required down payment, the interest rate, whether the lender is interested in lending to you and whether your application will be approved.

FUTURE

- Property type
- Property use

Residential properties may be owner-occupied, owner-occupied with a rental suite or used as a second home, a vacation home or an investment property (aka rental).

The buyer decides on a plan to use the property and the lender assesses the associated level of risk and cost of lending. The level of risk and cost determines the interest rates. For example, rentals property loans are higher risk for the lender, with higher costs, which leads to less competition and higher interest rates.

Down payment restrictions may also apply. Investment properties require a minimum down payment of 20%, with some lenders requiring 30% or more.

If the buyer is a non-resident, regardless of property use, the down payment requirements are typically 35% to 50%.

There are many unique situations that come up over property type and use, far too many to review here and now. Simply, the value of having access to multiple lenders enables mortgage brokers to find a fit and/or have the tools to build a case of why the property and borrower are a reasonable investment meeting common sense lending practices and objectives.

CHAPTER 7

First Comes Love,
Then Comes Mortgages

B y the spring of 2007, I was finally feeling completely settled back into my condo—just in time to get "twitterpated." (Bambi fans will recognize the term, but if you don't, picture sparkling cartoon hearts swirling around my head as I look dreamily into the distance.)

After reconnecting with my best friend of 10 years before, friendship became love. It was that quick, like a snap of the fingers.

That was in the spring, and in the fall, Mark moved in. We progressed as couples do. By February 2008, we were ready to buy a place together.

We found a two-year-old property on the outskirts of Richmond, one of the region's first geothermal buildings, in a quiet area with good access to the highway. Close to Mark's work, the location made for a convenient commute, and he'd been making the longer commute for almost a year. It was my turn.

On what felt like a whim, we made an offer less than a week after deciding to buy a place together, and it was accepted.

126   Now we had to arrange a mortgage. We reached out to the trusted broker who helped me when I bought my East Vancouver place, and he promptly lined up a variable five-year term at 5.15%, (prime rate minus 0.6%) with a 40-year amortization. (Note: 40-year amortizations are now extinct in Canada.)

The place became home to us immediately. In the evenings, with wineglasses in hand, we watched from our patio as the sun sank behind Vancouver Island. Incredible sunrises illuminated Mount Baker in the morning, and on winter nights, the brilliant lights of all three of the lower mainland's ski hills twinkled on the North Shore mountains. Mark's work was a seven-minute drive away. Our neighbours were amazing, there was a theatre within walking distance and we even had air conditioning to cool the hot summer nights. It was comfortable living.

Then it was time for me to head to Beijing, and we were apart for four months. We reconnected for the first time in the Venice airport for a family Mediterranean cruise celebrating Mark's parents' 30th wedding anniversary. It was a lovely trip. And while we were out at sea off the beautiful Italian coast, Mark proposed. On a windy, cool September night, wrapped in his oversized dress jacket and snuggled in his arms, I said yes.

Opting for a short engagement, we married the following April, celebrating in two of my favorite places in Vancouver, Queen Elizabeth Park and English Bay.

Then things changed again. Mark was hired for a great new position that extended his commute from seven minutes to about 45. And my commute—an hour in the morning and 90 minutes in the evening—wore on me. It became exhausting, and it was a big part of my day that I started to resent. A year and a half in, I was praying for change.

CHAPTER 8

Show Me the Money—The Mortgage Process

STEP 1	**STEP 2**	**STEP 3**	**STEP 4**	**STEP 5**
Application	Search/Submit	Commitment	Instructed	Completion

Although each client follows a similar process, each situation and file is a little bit different. Each client has varying degrees of knowledge, experience and interest in his or her mortgage. When clients come to a broker, they are also in different stages of life: refinancing for an upcoming renovation, renewing with a new lender; first-time buyers wanting to know what they can afford or investors looking to maximize their borrowing power; or possibly people in a jam looking for a financial solution they have almost given up on finding. Honestly, no two client files are the same.

"I must be your most difficult client," is something I've heard from many people. You're not. That's mortgages. They are difficult and there are lots to them. The challenge is educating clients when they are already knee deep in a purchase or refinance and dealing with compounded stresses. (Think back to the Holmes and Rahe Stress Scale!)

130   There are many pieces to a mortgage, and they all must come together to get it to completion. Just like putting together a puzzle, brokers gather the edge pieces of the picture first—the application and documentation. Once we have that, we can begin to fill in the rest for the approval: the property, the story and all the other team members needed to get to completion. For each step, there are key real estate team members who can help to make your experience effortless.

Like Jerry Maguire (queue my dream of being a sports agent), brokers are constantly working to "show you the money." To do this, we need your help. "Help us help you!"

STEP 1: APPLICATION

The application provides the basic personal and financial information necessary for assessing mortgage opportunities. It can often be completed online or over the phone in a 15- to 20-minute conversation. However, some brokers like to meet in person.

If your broker requests more information or the background on something, be as open, honest and detailed as you can. Be upfront about bankruptcies, consumer proposals and accounts that have been in collections as well as the properties you owned or own, whether you are separated or divorced and how many kids you have. The more the mortgage broker understands about you, the better equipped they are to position your file to lenders for the best mortgage options possible.

To ensure your broker has all the information required to help you get the best mortgage product for your needs, outline and share your short- and long-term financial, personal and professional goals as well.

Along with the application, the broker will need a signed agreement or a letter of engagement (or both) providing the necessary access to your credit history and your approval to complete the application. Supporting documents will also have to be provided to prepare the file for a mortgage approval or rate hold submission.

THE CLIENT AGREEMENT AND LETTER OF ENGAGEMENT

These documents outline how we will work together and give permission to share information and access your credit score. It acknowledges that the information provided in the mortgage application is true, complete and accurate and, along with the other information obtained, may be disclosed to potential mortgage lenders, insurers and related service providers such as your solicitor or realtor. Signing these documents does not commit you to a mortgage offer or to working exclusively with the mortgage broker.

DOCUMENTATION

When you complete an application, your broker will ask for your income, down payment and property documents, as detailed in earlier chapters.

Lenders may ask for other documentation as well, such as divorce certificates, property information on other properties you own, confirmation of your permanent residence and business financials.

If possible, provide all documents in PDF format by email. Apps such as TurboScan or SignNow can make this process easier.

MORTGAGE ASSESSMENT

With the application, documentation and credit details complete, an assessment of mortgage affordability can be calculated and provided. This will give you a game plan and a price range to begin your search or move forward with a refinance.

PRE-APPROVAL/RATE HOLD

If you're planning to search for a future purchase, your mortgage broker may request a pre-approval or rate hold, especially if interest rates are expected to rise.

There is a great deal of confusion, even within the industry, when it comes to pre-approvals and rate holds. Pre-approval is the commonly used term, but it is deceiving and its meaning has changed over time.

To issue a pre-approval in the past, an underwriter may have reviewed income and down payment documents, along with the initial application. The property and insurer's approval, if needed, was still required once there was an accepted offer.

The amount of time invested to pre-approve a file—a file that might never complete—was very costly for lenders, so they began to shift their practices. In many cases, pre-approvals are no longer offered by some lenders. Some have even bonused market rates. For example, if 2.89% is the current market rate, then the pre-approval rate could be 3.09% or even higher.

Once there is an accepted offer, if the current rate is lower than the pre-approval rate, the borrower is typically given the lower of the two rates. If rates increase, the borrower is protected with the pre-approved rate.

For lenders still offering pre-approvals at competitive market rates, there is very little upfront underwriting. They will not review documentation, and only a couple of lenders will review the application in some detail. A pre-approval commitment is issued only on the conditions of verification of income, down payment, property and insurer approval (if applicable). This documentation is only reviewed once an accepted offer is available.

Another term used in the industry is rate holds. This is where a client file is submitted and zero underwriting is completed—so basically, most pre-approvals and rate holds are the same today. It's a computerized approval (or decline), giving you access to the pre-approved rate for a hold term, usually 90 or 120 days.

However, rate hold is also a term used with a mortgage approval. When a **133** borrower is approved, they are guaranteed their rate until completion or until expiry, usually 90 to 120 days.

Mortgage brokers must rely on their knowledge of each lender's guidelines on income and down payment requirements. Having the required documents at the outset is very important for the broker to ensure the pre-approval or rate hold submission is as accurate as possible.

Ultimately, there is no official "pre-approval" to go buy anything under the sun. Pre-approvals and rate holds are not guarantees that the lender will approve a mortgage.

The property always factors into the lender's decision, so the underwriting that matters will not take place until you've made an offer and it's been accepted on a specific property.

This is why subject-free offers come with sizable risks, which you will learn more about in Chapter 15.

Pre-builds (new builds) come with unique consideration for holding rates since closing dates could be months or possibly years from the signed contract. When considering a pre-build, it is best to discuss with your mortgage broker on how to prepare and protect yourself for the risks associated with purchasing a property that does not currently exist.

Similarly, construction financing requires a much different file review and set up. If you plan to buy and build, or you own land and want to build, review the details with your broker. Lender options and the mortgage structure vary greatly.

YOUR TEAM

Mortgage Broker

Your mortgage broker works for and with you to help you get the approval you need to finance a purchase or to complete a refinance, renewal or switch.

134   Brokers have access to hundreds of mortgage products from a variety of lenders, each with their own niche in the marketplace. Knowing your needs and objectives, he or she searches the market to find solutions that fit.

As independent agents, they are in the position to truly work for your best interest. They have no ties to shareholder demands or sales targets.

And the best part is that lenders cover the cost of their services, paying a finder's fee for each new mortgage.

STEP 2: HOME SEARCH & APPLICATION SUBMISSION

RENEWAL, REFINANCE OR SWITCH

In the case of a renewal, refinance or a switch from a current lender to a new one, a broker would provide options based on the details from your application, income documents and property information. Once a suitable lender and product is determined, the application can be submitted for approval.

PURCHASE

If you are purchasing, a property needs to be selected first before an approval submission can go in.

When looking for a property it is recommended to buy based on your budget. You should have a good idea of what this would look like from the mortgage assessment provided to you by your broker.

Budget

Rather than reinvent the wheel here, I think budgeting is best outsourced to CMHC's free step-by-step guide. In Step 2, page 5 in the Homebuying Guide and page 4 in Workbook and Checklist, there is an easy-to-follow budgeting process and form. It's a fantastic resource tool that can be downloaded from *cmhc.ca/stepbystep*.

Offer to Purchase

Once you have found your home, you will work with your realtor to prepare an offer. This will include the purchase price, your deposit amount and any requests about "chattels" (i.e., movable property contents of the home such as appliances and drapes, or things like plants on the property). It will also state your subjects (conditions for purchase) and the subject removal, closing and possession dates.

IMPORTANT! It's important to note that the deposit is different than the down payment. Your deposit amount will eventually go towards your total down payment; however, it is required immediately, usually within 24 hours of subject removal. In subject-free offers, the deposit may be present along with the offer.

The down payment isn't required until you meet with your solicitor near your closing date.

To complete your offer and remove subjects, you need to ensure you have the deposit amount readily available. Otherwise, your offer could be considered invalid even after being accepted.

The deposit is money representing the seriousness of your intention to buy the property. If subjects are removed and you then back out, the deposit is non-refundable. The seller also has the option to pursue legal action.

If the property has any "unique" aspects, the lender options may be limited. For example, if the property is on leasehold land, has age restrictions, there are special assessments pending or water leaks, it's a remediated grow-op, contains vermiculite or asbestos; is commercial, mixed or otherwise unique zoning, if there is livestock present, etc., it will be important to discuss the situation with your mortgage broker before making an offer.

If your offer is accepted by the seller, you or your realtor will need to forward the contract of purchase and sale (CPS) to your mortgage broker, along with the MLS listing and the property disclosure statement (PDS). If it is a strata property, you'll also need the strata form B, depreciation report and annual general meeting (AGM) minutes.

If you wish to make a subject-free offer, the property documents are usually made available for your review. Ensure your mortgage broker has copies before making a subject-free offer.

Based on the details of the contract of purchase and sale, the mortgage file is prepared for submission to the lender. If the product options have already been discussed, the mortgage broker may submit the file immediately. Otherwise, lender and product options may now be considered with property and contract details in mind.

YOUR TEAM

Realtor

One of the most important investments you can make in real estate is finding a great realtor. An all-star realtor can be the difference between investing well and building wealth or investing poorly and losing your hard-earned money. Take the time to find someone who is experienced, knowledgeable about the areas you're interested in and demonstrates their commitment to you through their work on your behalf. It will make a difference to your bottom line.

For example, a downtown Vancouver realtor will know the ins and outs and pros and cons of its various condo buildings and developers. A realtor from Mission, familiar with Mission's housing market, may not be as educated about downtown Vancouver. That lack of familiarity could result in future surprise assessments, costing not only money but a great deal of stress as well.

I recommend connecting with two to four realtors to get a feel for their style of business before making your decision. Be honest with them that you are in the process of sourcing a realtor and they can determine if they have the time to meet with you. You could spend a lot of time with this person, so it's important you're comfortable.

137

I have interviewed trusted realtors on my blog (irenestrong.com/category/realtor-profile/). I can provide a list of agents I think may be top considerations based on your location and personality fit.

Mortgage Broker

Once you've identified a realtor, introduce him or her to your mortgage broker by email. This relationship is important in ensuring the offer and financing are aligned and important details are not missed.

As you identify properties of interest, provide your mortgage broker with the MLS listing number or property details. He or she will help you accurately project mortgage affordability and costs specific to that property. Different property tax levels, building maintenance fees and other factors can have an impact on your overall affordability and can vary dramatically from one property to the next.

Home Inspector

A home inspection is not required by lenders or insurers, but it can provide valuable information that may influence whether you carry through with an offer or not. Inspectors perform detailed evaluations of all the building's interior and exterior components and systems. They identify deficiencies that represent a substantial investment or a danger to the dwelling's occupants. They will note the probability of problems based on the current design and point out issues that are likely to be difficult to maintain on an ongoing basis. Inspectors are trained to look for secondary signs that can indicate issues even if no visible signs are present.

STEP 1
Application

STEP 2
Search/Submit

STEP 3
Commitment

STEP 4
Instructed

STEP 5
Completion

STEP 3: MORTGAGE COMMITMENT

138

Depending on market conditions, approval can take anywhere from a few hours to two weeks or more. The approval comes in the form of a document called a **mortgage commitment**, which outlines the terms and conditions of the mortgage, including the loan amount, insurance premium (if applicable), interest rate, term, amortization, payment amount and payment frequency. The closing and maturity dates should be noted, along with the conditions the borrower and solicitor need to meet. Additional documents may be required, along with the signing of the commitment, completion of a pre-authorized deposit (PAD) form, a void cheque, identification and solicitor contact details. The commitment may also include a request for an appraisal.

LINGO!

MORTGAGE COMMITMENT (MORTGAGE APPROVAL)

The mortgage approval from the lender, which outlines the mortgage details and conditions to be met for final approval and funding.

Mortgage commitments vary vastly from lender to lender. There is not one consistent layout required in the industry. All commitments will provide mortgage details (rate, term, amortization and payment) and the conditions. Some will include the prepayment privileges and other lender provisions.

The mortgage commitment is a contract between you and the lender. If something doesn't make sense, ask questions. I also recommend taking a copy of the signed or most recent commitment to the solicitor's appointment to ensure the numbers match. If something is off, contact your broker immediately. The commitment passes through many hands before it arrives to the solicitor and there are many opportunities for human error to occur, especially when it comes to the numbers.

PAYMENT SCHEDULE

The commitment will note how the payments are currently set up: monthly, semi-monthly, biweekly accelerated, weekly accelerated, etc. You can change this selection when you sign the commitment or at the appointment with your solicitor. In most cases, you may also change the payment schedule after the mortgage has been funded, but each lender has different rules governing payment schedule changes once repayment is underway.

The accelerated payment options allow a borrower to make one additional monthly payment a year, which effectively lowers the overall remaining amortization by approximately two to 3.5 years over a five-year term.

To illustrate the difference between the payment options, let's take an example of a $1,000 monthly payment and adjust it for each of the payment options:

MONTHLY PAYMENT
$1,000 monthly payment
12 payments a year
$12,000 paid annually

SEMI-MONTHLY PAYMENT
$1,000 monthly payments / 2 = $500 payment
24 payments a year
$12,000 paid annually

BIWEEKLY NON-ACCELERATED PAYMENT

$12,000 annual payments / 26 payments = $461.54 payment

26 payments a year

$12,000 paid annually

WEEKLY NON-ACCELERATED PAYMENT

$12,000 annual payments / 52 payments = $230.77 payment

52 payments a year

$12,000 paid annually

BIWEEKLY ACCELERATED PAYMENT

$1,000 monthly payments / 2 = $500 payment

26 payments a year

$13,000 paid annually

WEEKLY ACCELERATED PAYMENT

$1,000 monthly payments / 4 = $250 payment

52 payments a year

$13,000 paid annually

CONDITIONS

Along with the mortgage application, most or all the income, property and down payment documents are packaged and sent to the **underwriter** or **fulfillment specialist** to verify the application details. Before you remove the subjects on your offer, it's important that the mortgage broker has all conditions "satisfied" or approved.

LINGO!

UNDERWRITER

The person who reviews and approves (or rejects) mortgage and other loan applications. The underwriter may also be responsible for reviewing all the documentation provided, to verify the applicant's details. They are the gatekeeper for the lender and aim to approve only the files that meet the lender's guidelines.

FULFILLMENT SPECIALIST

A person who may assist an underwriter in reviewing the documentation (for income, down payment and property) provided by borrowers to meet the conditions of a mortgage commitment.

IMPORTANT! During the application process, delays in providing information can end up being very costly. Your mortgage broker relies on you to promptly provide any information that may be requested by a lender and to ensure the information you provide is accurate and complete.

LENDER-APPROVED SOLICITORS AND APPRAISERS

Solicitors and appraisers must be approved by the lender, and if the solicitor is not accepted, a new solicitor must be found and their contact information provided. Lenders will require the solicitor's name, company name, and complete contact details.

If an appraisal is required, the borrower is typically responsible for paying the charges. The mortgage broker is responsible for making the order arrangements.

PROPERTY TAXES

The commitment will usually note who will be responsible for the payment of property tax. Depending on the file and lender, some borrowers must pay through the lender. Some lenders do not have a tax account option so borrowers must pay their taxes to the municipality themselves.

Lender's tax accounts can be a benefit. It can be one less thing to remember to save up for and to pay, especially if the tax bill is in the thousands annually.

If the amount is less than $1,000 and can be easily managed with a lump-sum payment to the municipality, it could save you time and hassle that comes with dealing with the lender's tax account.

Challenges with lender tax accounts can include:

1. In some cases, lenders have set a standard national percentage they use to determine the tax payment. For cities such as Vancouver where property taxes are lower than the national average, the tax account may require overpayment, sometimes nearly double. Adjustments can be made, but sometime there will be excess funds sitting in your tax account rather than in your personal bank account.

2. Depending on the closing date of your purchase or refinance, there may not be enough money in the tax account by the tax due date. The lender will issue a notice and your monthly payments will increase going forward to make up the shortfall, plus an estimated inflation increase for the following year. This can have a substantial impact on your future payments.

3. Some lenders require the borrower to contact them in the first year to register their property tax account. If you fail to do so, the result could be that the taxes are not paid, and you end up in arrears.

4. If you forget that the lender is paying the taxes and make a payment to the municipality, it can cost an administration fee and take months to get a refund.

COLLATERAL CHARGE

Mortgages from banks and credit unions have a collateral charge. A **collateral charge** is a way of securing a loan against your property. Unlike a traditional mortgage, a loan secured by a collateral mortgage is re-advanceable and can be registered at a higher amount than your current mortgage amount. Some lenders allow you to select the amount for which you register your mortgage, which can be upwards of 150% of the appraised property value. By registering at the higher value, you can save on future legal and discharge fees if you want to increase your loan. The increase would still be subject to credit approval and appraisal.

The downside to a collateral charge is that other lenders don't usually accept transfers or switches of mortgages with collateral charges. If you want to move to a new lender, this can mean legal fees. Also, if you have other debts such as a line of credit or credit card with the same lender and they are not in good standing, those missed payments could be linked to your overall client file with the lender and potentially cause a default on your home mortgage.

143

LINGO!

COLLATERAL CHARGE

Unlike a standard mortgage, a collateral charge is re-advanceable. That is, once you've paid back a portion of the original loan, or if you haven't taken out the full amount accessible, or the property value has increased, the lender can review and lend additional funds without additional solicitor fees.

Appraisal and qualifying processes are still required, but a collateral charge mortgage could save you the larger fees of a refinance.

The positive aspect of a collateral charge is not having to pay new legal fees if you want to access more equity from your home. The negative, if your mortgage and other debts (say, a line of credit or credit card) are with the same lender and your other debts are not in good standing, those missed payments can be linked to your mortgage account and cause a default on all your borrowing with the bank, including your home mortgage.

Also, if you want to switch lenders later (with no changes to the amount or amortization), you may not be able to without completing a refinance and paying legal fees to re-register the property. In typical switch programs (from mortgages not registered as collateral charges), lenders usually cover the legal fees.

PREPAYMENT PRIVILEGE OPTIONS

Most lenders state prepayment privilege options in their cost of credit disclosure, which appears in their commitment letter and/or in a statement provided when you meet with your solicitor. If these options are not listed, ensure your broker advises you on the details, including maximums and minimums as well as date restrictions.

144

In addition to prepayment privileges, you will also want to know what your prepayment penalties will be. These are usually three months interest or an interest rate differential (IRD) calculation. Some lenders may have other prepayment penalties depending on the type of product you select. You will want to know what these are before signing your commitment.

COMMITMENT SAMPLES

There is no standard guideline for a mortgage commitment. Each lender presents the information in a slightly different format.

I have provided four samples to give you an idea of what you might expect: from a bank, a monoline lender, a B lender and a private lender. These samples show the varying degrees of information provided, ranging from two pages to eight pages. The longest, the eight-page monoline lender commitment, usually includes additional pages on the cost of borrowing disclosure and pre-authorized debit information. The two-page document from the private lender has little to no legal jargon and isn't nearly as involved as the other lenders' requirements.

On the bank sample, I have made some notes and highlighted key areas for reference. These are keys areas addressed in the signing package, along with other discussion points. Your mortgage broker may present and review these with you by email, telephone, in person or a through a combination of these communications and meetings.

SAMPLE: COMMITMENT
Bank

BANK LENDER

To:	From:
C/O:	

Application ID: Date Issued:

Property Address:

We are pleased to confirm that your application has been approved under the following terms and conditions.

Basic Loan Amount	$360,000.00	Advance Date	
Insurance Premium	$0.00	Term	5 year Closed
Total Loan Amount	$360,000.00	Amortization	30 years
Interest Rate	2.69%	Monthly Payment	$1,455.42
See Interest Rate Section for more information		(Principal + Interest Only)	
Interest Rate Set Date	Already Set	Taxes to be paid	
Guarantor(s)			

Payment Frequency or First Payment Date Options (Selection is mandatory):

Payment Frequency Options listed below are for new mortgage(s) only. Payment amount **does not** include tax portion if taxes are to be paid through

Please Note: Any changes to the Advance Date may result in a change to your first mortgage payment date and any change will be reflected in the Mortgage Repayment Terms Confirmation Notice you will receive shortly after your Advance Date. Please ensure sufficient funds are available in your bank account to cover the mortgage payment.

☐ $1,455.42 Monthly payments _____ within 30 days after the Closing Date excluding 29th, 30th, or 31st of the month

☐ $727.71 Bi-weekly payments on every second _____ within 16 days after the Closing date (Mon – Fri only).

☐ $363.86 Weekly payments on every _____ within 9 days after Closing Date (Mon – Fri only).

☐ $727.71 Semi-monthly payments on _____ either the 1st or 15th, whichever comes first after the Closing date.

PREPAYMENT POLICIES

Prepayment

Our standard prepayment privileges apply.   Full details on prepayment privileges,   Options
can be obtained from your servicing branch.

INTEREST RATE

Rate

We guarantee you our Fixed Annual interest rate(s) and term(s) until   .   If this is a blended interest rate, the new
reduced or reset interest rate applies to the new term only.

Fixed Annual Interest Rate guarantee of 2.69%

CONDITIONS OF APPROVAL

Mortgage Payment Setup

Before we submit the mortgage documents to your solicitor you are required to meet with a Client Solutions Advisor or Financial
Advisor at the   branch of your choice to set up your mortgage payment details.   will contact you to schedule this
meeting. Please bring two (2) pieces of identification, one of which is government issued photo identification, to this meeting.

Offer and Listing

You are to provide a copy of the complete signed and accepted purchase agreement and, if applicable, the Multiple Listing Service
(MLS) agreement.

SAMPLE: COMMITMENT
Bank Cont'd

Application ID:	Property:	Issued:

Owner Occupied Property
You must occupy the subject property as your principal residence.

Downpayment - Gift Letter
You are to provide us with a gift letter, satisfactory to us, from an immediate family member confirming a gift of $20,000.00.

Downpayment - Own Resources
You are to provide us with verification, satisfactory to us, that $70,000.00 for the down payment is available from your own resources. You must provide 30 days of history. If the funds are held in one or more deposit accounts, you must provide the most recent account history for each account. We may ask for additional account history.

Income
Verification is to be provided by way of a recent paystub or notification of pay deposit dated no earlier than 60 days before the application date and any one of the following:
- Signed letter on employers letterhead, or
- Two most recent bank statements showing direct payroll deposits, or
- T4 for the most recent tax year, or
- Notice of Assessment with T1 General/ CRA my Account Assessment for the most recent tax year.
  in the amount of $72,500.00

SOLICITOR / NOTARY CONDITIONS

Title Insurance Requirement
Your solicitor will advise you if title insurance is required to complete this transaction, if title insurance is required all costs incurred will be your responsibility.

Title Insurance Required
Title insurance is mandatory for all mortgages on properties located in British Columbia. We will instruct your Solicitor/Notary to submit to us a lender's Title Insurance policy. You are responsible to pay your Solicitor/Notary for this service.

Solicitor
This transaction will be completed by a solicitor/notary. We will instruct the solicitor/notary upon receipt of acceptance of this conditional approval and the requested information. For refinance transactions, the solicitor/notary will be responsible to pay out existing debts from the mortgage proceeds.

GENERAL CONDITIONS

Condition Fulfillment
You will pay all fees associated with arranging this mortgage, which includes any legal, survey, appraisal, and insurance mortgage costs.
All costs incurred to arrange this mortgage are your responsibility.

Appraisal
will obtain an appraisal report to ensure all property requirements are met.

Due on sale
You may have to pay back immediately all the money you owe us under this mortgage if you sell, transfer, or mortgage the property. Immediate payout may also be required if you default on this mortgage. If we decide immediate payout is not required, all payment obligations remain the same.

Portability
You may be able to port your mortgage, with its rates and terms, and move it to another property. This is called porting a mortgage. Speak to your servicing branch to find out if you can port your mortgage.

Signed Commitment
Return to us this signed Commitment Letter (and Bridge Loan Commitment Letter if applicable), and Solicitor/Notary information.

All borrowers and guarantors, as applicable, are required to sign the acceptance page of this commitment and return it to us by

Yours truly,

Broker Relationship Manager,

SAMPLE: COMMITMENT
Bank Cont'd

Application ID:	Property:		Issued:

CUSTOMER AUTHORIZATION / ACKNOWLEDGEMENT

In this Commitment Letter, "we", "our" and "us" mean any _____ Group Member or the collective _____ Group and include any program or joint venture any of these parties participates in; "you" and "your" mean the borrower and co-borrower(s) (if applicable) and guarantor(s) (if applicable). "Service" means any personal banking, insurance, brokerage or financial product or service offered by us. You agree that all information that you give us will, at any time, be true and

We may collect your personal information, use it, and disclose it to any person or organization in order to: confirm your identity, understand your needs, determine your eligibility for our Services, satisfy applicable legal and regulatory requirements, manage and assess our risks; and prevent or detect fraud or criminal activity. We may keep and use information about you for as long as it is needed for the purposes described in this Commitment Letter.

In addition, we may offer you Services that we think may be of interest to you, and give information about you to other members of the _____ Group so that these companies may tell you directly about their Services. Your consent to this is not a condition of doing business with us and you may withdraw it at any time.

When you apply for, accept, or guarantee a loan or credit facility or otherwise become indebted to us, we may use, give to, obtain, verify, share and exchange financial, credit and other information about you with others including your employer, credit bureaus, mortgage insurers, creditor insurers, reinsurers, registries, other companies in the _____ Group, Investigative Bodies such as the Bank Crime Prevention and Investigation Office and other persons with whom you may have financial dealings, as well as any other person as may be permitted or required by law. We may do this throughout the relationship we have with you. You authorize any person whom we contact in this regard to provide such information to us.

We may ask you for your SIN to verify and report credit information to credit bureaus and credit reporting agencies as well as to confirm your identity. You may refuse to consent to its use or disclosure for purposes other than as required by law.

We do not provide directly all the services related to your relationship with us. We may use third party service providers to process or handle personal information on our behalf and to assist us with various services. Some of our service providers are located outside of Canada. As a result, your personal information may be accessible to regulatory authorities in accordance with the law of these jurisdictions. When personal information is provided to our service providers, we will require them to protect the information in a manner that is consistent with _____ Group privacy policies and practices.

Third Party Determination - By signing this Commitment Letter you confirm that the product(s) and/or service(s) offered to you herein will not be used for or on behalf of any individual or entity other than you and the other parties named in the Commitment Letter for whose benefit such products and services are intended unless information about such individuals or entities was previously disclosed to the Bank on a _____ Group Third Party Determination form.

Solicitor/Notary Contact Information

Name:	Firm Name:
Address:	
Phone:	Fax:

Any disclosure statement in connection with the loan you are applying for will be given at the time that you enter into the Personal Credit Agreement

Consent to receive electronic communications by initialing below:

I allow The _____ and other members of the _____ group of companies listed below _____ Members") to send me electronic messages (such as emails) about their products and services, offers, events and other valuable information as well as information about the products and services of other trusted partners that may be of interest to me.

I understand I can unsubscribe from receiving such messages at any time. If I do, I understand I may still receive certain electronic messages from Members as permitted by law, such as transactional messages relating to my existing accounts and services

This consent is being sought on behalf of each _____ which includes any company(ies) or person(s) that form a part of the group of companies in the future

SAMPLE: COMMITMENT
Bank Cont'd

148

Application ID:	Property:	Issued:

Applicable in the Province of Quebec only: It is the express wish of the parties that this Authorization and all documents relating to it be drawn up and executed in English. Les parties conviennent et exigent expressément que ce contrat et tous les documents qui s'y rapportent soient rédigés en anglais.

Each borrower is entitled to receive separate agreements and cost of borrowing disclosure documents related to the account(s). All agreements and cost of borrowing disclosures related to the account(s) will be sent to the address of the primary borrower and separate documents will also be sent to each co-borrower at his/her address that appears in our records. This includes the initial disclosure statement and credit agreement, as well as all subsequent periodic statements, agreements, disclosure or other notices related to the account(s).
Alternatively, a co-borrower may consent to all documentation being provided on his/her behalf by providing it only once to the address of the primary borrower.
The co-borrower agrees that we may rely on this consent through all subsequent extensions, renewals and amendments related to the account(s), until such time as the co-borrower gives us notice in writing that he/she wishes to change his/her disclosure preference. A co-borrower may change his/her disclosure preference at any time in the future by contacting his/her Scotiabank branch.
If you have consented to all documentation being provided on your behalf by providing it only once to the address of the primary borrower, this is reflected below by checking "Disclosure - No" next to your name.
Each co-borrower acknowledges that he/she has been advised of his/her ability to receive separate disclosure and any checking of "Disclosure - No" next to his/her name below reflects his/her wishes.

The terms and conditions detailed in this mortgage commitment are hereby accepted this _____ day of _____, 20_____.

_____

SAMPLE: COMMITMENT
Monoline Lender

MONOLINE LENDER

Dear

Thank you for choosing   for your financing needs. This letter and its terms and conditions represent Service Corporation's commitment to you. For purposes of this letter   may also be referred to as ' "we", "us" or "our". We look forward to working with you to help fulfill your financing needs. Your Mortgage details are as follows:

Mortgage Number:	
Name of Borrower(s):	
Name of Guarantor(s)/ Covenantor(s):	N / A
Address of Property to be Mortgaged & Legal Description:	
Mailing Address of Borrower:	

Principal Amount:		
Basic Mortgage Amount:	$558,000.00	
	$17,298.00	Mortgage default insurance premium, if applicable. Borrower will pay GST/PST/HST if applicable.
Total Principal Amount:	$575,298.00	

Charge Type/ Priority Ranking:		1st Charge
Interest Rate:	2.00%	This is a variable rate based on the Prime Rate -0.70%
Regularly Scheduled Payment Amount:	$2,436.11	Payable commencing on the First Regular Payment Date. Your Monthly payment includes Principal and interest and is based on the Interest Rate. Your Monthly payment may be increased by additional components for property taxes and other applicable amounts. If you wish to change your payment frequency, please complete the payment frequency change section in this letter. All payments are automatically withdrawn by us when due, from the bank account you instruct us to take the payments from. If you have not already done so, please complete our Pre-Authorized Debit (PAD) Agreement and provide a void cheque with the acceptance of this Commitment Letter.
Property Taxes:	$1,391.00	Paid by Borrower

Dates and Time Periods

Acceptance Date:		Date by which you must communicate to us your acceptance of the terms of this letter
Funding Requirements Date:		Date by which borrower conditions to fund the Mortgage must be satisfied
Advance Date:		
Interest Adjustment Date:		
First Regular Payment Date:		
Maturity Date:		
Term:	Closed - 5 Years	
Amortization:	25 Years	

OR-030-031E   Borrower(s)/ Guarantor(s) Initials

SAMPLE: COMMITMENT
Monoline Cont'd

WHAT WE REQUIRE TO FUND THE MORTGAGE

In order to close this Mortgage, each Borrower/Guarantor will be required to present at the closing of this Mortgage, original, valid, legible Canadian photo ID, that is in good condition. Failure to meet   individual ID requirements will nullify this Commitment Letter and result in the cancellation of this Mortgage application.

In order to advance the Principal Amount on the Advance Date, we require the following to be completed to our satisfaction on or prior to the Funding Requirements Date unless otherwise specified below:

1. Confirmation of down payment of $62,000.00 and closing costs of $9300 Require 90 day history of account statements to confirm value
2. Fully executed Agreement of Purchase and Sale along with the MLS listing for

3. Copy of valid Work Visa, satisfactory to us.
4.   : Confirmation of total annual income broken down as follows: Salaried income of $68,378.94. Require current job letter and pay stub and 2015/2016 NOA?s/T4 if income is not guaranteed or using bonuses and/or overtime
5.   : Confirmation of total annual income of $48,561.89, broken down as follows: 1) Self-Employed income of $5,837.33 Require 2 years NOA's with corresponding T1 Generals with Statement of Business Activities. 2)Other income of $42,724.56. Require current job letter and pay stub *** RECD 2015/2016 T1 GEN & SBA / REQUIRE CORRESPONDING NOA'S & LOE AND PAYSTUB ***
6. Contact information for the Solicitor/Notary who will be acting on your behalf for this deal is required.
7. Receipt of a signed Pre-Authorized Debit Agreement and either a void cheque or proof of account ownership for automatic payments is required.
8. Receipt of signed Commitment Letter and Additional Provisions within 10 calendar days of commitment date is required.
9.   : Require current mortgage statement to confirm balance of $255,196 w/payment of $988.54 m(required) and confirmation of property taxes of $1268 yr(required) and condo fees of $265mo(required) and rental income of $1600 mo(recd)
10. Property TaxesRequire current property tax assessment to confirm 2017 property taxes

Also, please note the following will have to be completed and received by   3 Business Days prior to (unless otherwise stated) the Advance Date in order for   to advance the Principal Amount on the Advance Date:

1. Solicitor/ Notary to provide (i) the Identification Verification and Attestation Requirements for Individuals together with the photocopies (front and back) of the primary identification and (ii) the Solicitors Interim Report and Requisition For Mortgage Advance no less than 3 Business Days before the Advance Date. Drafts of these documents are included in the Solicitor's (or Notary's) Instructions package issued after acceptance of the Commitment Letter. Borrowers (including any Guarantors) hereby specifically authorize the Solicitor / Notary to provide photo and other personal identification to
2. Solicitor/ Notary to provide a acceptable Strata Form B
3. Title Insurance is REQUIRED. Solicitor/ Notary to provide   a copy of Title Insurance Certificate prior to closing. Full Conveyance Title Insurance Package will be required from either First Canadian Title, Stewart Title or Chicago Title. The cost is the responsibility of the Borrower(s).
4. Solicitor/ Notary to register Mortgage in the name of:
          . A copy of the prepared charge/mortgage must be provided for our review prior to funding.
5. A copy of the prepared charge/mortgage must be provided for our review prior to funding.

When you have accepted and returned this Commitment Letter to us and when we have received the required information from yourself or your authorized representative, we will instruct the Solicitor/ Notary to commence work on your transaction.

Advance of Funds:

On the Advance Date, and subject to meeting the requirements to fund the Mortgage, we will forward to the Solicitor/ Notary the net funds estimated at $558,000.00 as calculated in the Cost of Borrowing Disclosure Summary.

Note: This is an estimate at this point in time and is subject to change prior to closing.

You are also responsible for paying the legal fees and associated costs charged by the Solicitor/ Notary. You have advised us (or will advise us as soon as possible) that the Solicitor/ Notary's contact information is:

Name: _____   Address: _____

Firm Name: _____   _____

SAMPLE: COMMITMENT
Monoline Cont'd

Email:

Phone: Fax:

Because the Solicitor/ Notary you have selected represents   , as well as yours, we reserve the right to engage independent counsel, if we choose to do so. All fees and costs for the independent counsel would be your responsibility. If we have any concerns with respect to the Solicitor/ Notary you have selected, we will contact you as soon as possible.

Mortgage Provisions:

Your approved Mortgage contains provisions specific to the   **Mortgage** product. These additional provisions are appended to this letter and will be registered on title along with the Standard Charge/ Mortgage Terms.

For applicable details and conditions and fees and penalties related to these features of your Mortgage, please see the Additional Provisions, the attached Cost of Borrowing Disclosure Summary and/or contact your Mortgage Broker for details. After your Mortgage has been funded by   one of our Customer Service Representatives will be glad to assist you in relation to any questions you may have concerning your Mortgage.

We thank you in advance for your business.

Yours Truly,

YOUR ACKNOWLEDGEMENTS, CONSENTS AND ACCEPTANCE

Personal Information:

You acknowledge that we may:

1. Collect from and confirm with various sources, your identity, financial and other personal information (Personal Information) during the course of your relationship with us. These sources may include: credit reporting agencies, your mortgage broker, government registries, employer(s), other financial institutions, references that you may provide to us, and other sources we consider appropriate. We also collect information from your various transactions and financial behaviour with us and our business associates.
2. Disclose and exchange your Personal Information with credit reporting agencies and financial institutions. This may include mortgage insurers such as CMHC, Genworth, Canada Guaranty or others.
3. Use your Personal Information to identify or locate you, protect you and us from fraud and error, determine eligibility for the Mortgage and your ongoing creditworthiness. We may also use your Personal Information to administer your Mortgage, provide ongoing service, and comply with legal and regulatory requirements.
4. Disclose and exchange your Personal Information with any entity, or prospective entity, who funds, purchases, invests in or takes an assignment of all or part of the Mortgage (or who otherwise considers doing so). We may also disclose and exchange your Personal Information with any entity that supplies us with administration services related to the Mortgage.

Unless you contact us to withdraw your consent, you agree that we may:

a. Use your Personal Information to understand your financial needs and eligibility for additional or future products and services so we may tell you about or recommend or offer products and services that may meet your needs or be of interest to you, through direct mail, e-mail, telephone and/ or other means.
b. Share your Personal Information within the   group of companies so that others in our group may tell you about, recommend or offer their products and services.
c. Share your Personal Information with third parties   has selected and made arrangements with as its business associates, for credit and payment card services, insurance and home ownership related products and services. These third parties may directly or through us determine your eligibility for and tell you about or offer you their products and services.

You may contact us at

SAMPLE: COMMITMENT
Monoline Cont'd

1. Obtain access to the Personal Information we hold about you at any time, to review accuracy of the content, and to have it amended if required.
2. Withdraw your consent to items a), b) and/ or c) above.

All Personal Information is collected, maintained and used by   and its business associates and service providers in accordance with the   Privacy Code, which is available to you at

ACCEPTANCE

This Commitment Letter is open for acceptance until the Acceptance Date. Please sign below, initial each page of this Commitment Letter, and return it to us prior to the Acceptance Date. This Commitment Letter will supersede and replace any Commitment Letter that had been previously issued by us to you in relation to the applicable Mortgage.

When you enter into the Mortgage, the Loan and the obligations of the Borrower(s) and Guarantor(s) thereunder, will be governed by the Commitment Letter, the Additional Provisions, the Mortgage, and the Standard Charge/Mortgage Terms. If there is any inconsistency or conflict between the provisions in these documents, the provisions of these documents shall apply in the following order of precedence to resolve the conflict or inconsistency: (i) the Commitment Letter; (ii) the Additional Provisions; (iii) the Mortgage; and (iv) the Standard Charge/Mortgage Terms.

Capitalized terms not defined in this Commitment Letter are defined in the Additional Provisions or Standard Charge/ Mortgage Terms. You may find a copy of the Standard Charge/ Mortgage Terms that will apply to your Mortgage on-line at

Any reference to "letter", "Loan Agreement", "Commitment Letter" or "Commitment" means a reference to this letter.

By accepting this Commitment Letter, I acknowledge that:

- This Mortgage is for my benefit, and is not for the benefit of any undisclosed third-party;
- This letter is personal to me and may not be transferred;
- That all representations made by me/us, and all information submitted by me/us or the Mortgage Broker in connection with the Mortgage application, is true and accurate; and
- I   may decline to advance all or any portion of the Mortgage if there are any errors, omissions or misrepresentations in relation to my application or information otherwise becomes available to   which is inconsistent with the information used to underwrite the Mortgage.

Cost of Borrowing Disclosure:

Attached to this letter is a Cost of Borrowing Disclosure Summary (the "Summary") which contains information in respect of your mortgage approval. This Summary sets out a brief description of the amount of money we are lending you, the cost of borrowing it, and some of the terms and conditions of your Mortgage. At least 3 Business Days prior to the Advance Date, you will have to meet with your Solicitor/Notary to review and execute a Cost of Borrowing Disclosure Statement (the "Statement") that provides the full details concerning the cost of borrowing (and the Statement shall replace the Summary). If you fail to execute and return the Statement less than two (2) business days before the advance of funds by   ', you consent to waive the two (2) day notice requirement. By accepting this Commitment Letter, the Borrower(s) consent to us providing a single copy of all cost of borrowing disclosures to only one (and not all of the) Borrower(s), and not to the Guarantor(s). You may withdraw your consent in writing, at any time. Please keep this Statement received from the Solicitor/Notary as it will help you understand your rights and obligations under the Mortgage.

I hereby acknowledge receipt of the Summary. I have not yet signed the Mortgage, otherwise entered into an obligation under the Mortgage or made any payment under the Mortgage.

☐ I have lived in Canada for less than 5 years (check if yes).   ☐ I have lived in Canada for less than 5 years (check if yes).
☐ I have not owned or co-owned a residential unit in Canada in   ☐ I have not owned or co-owned a residential unit in Canada in
    the last 4 years (check if yes).   the last 4 years (check if yes).

_____   _____   _____   _____
(Applicant)   Date   (Applicant)   Date

Electronic Communication:

OR-030-031E   Borrower(s)/ Guarantor(s) Initials

SAMPLE: COMMITMENT
Monoline Cont'd

Transactional Messages: At _____ , we continue to strive to be paperless. To contact you electronically with transactional messages and alerts concerning your mortgage account, please provide your email address.

_____
Email Address

_____
Email Address

Commercial Messages: In order for us to send you product and service information (in addition to transactional messages regarding your account), Canadian Anti-Spam law and regulations require you to provide consent prior to receiving Commercial Marketing Messages in electronic format. Accordingly, do you agree to receive emails from _____ which may contain marketing information? You can unsubscribe at any time.

Please check this box if you agree to receive this information electronically from _____

☐ I, _____ , agree to receive information at the above email address.
☐ I, _____ , agree to receive information at the above email address.

Payment Frequency Change Request:

Your Regularly Scheduled Payments will occur on a Monthly basis. If you wish to change this, please select one of the options below and complete the corresponding information. You will receive a letter after the Advance Date confirming the amount and dates of your Regularly Scheduled Payments and the interest adjustment amount caused by the change below, if applicable. Please note that an interest adjustment amount will apply if your First Regular Payment Date is more than one payment frequency after your Advance Date. For details, refer to the Standard Charge/ Mortgage Terms.

☐ Weekly: Day of Week: _____ (Monday-Friday only)
(First Regular Payment Date will be 7-13 days after Advance Date. If the
First Regular Payment Date is more than 7 days after the Advance Date
an interest adjustment amount will be required.)

  ☐ Accelerated
  ☐ Non-Accelerated
  (Weekly/Bi-Weekly only)

☐ Bi-Weekly: Requested First Regular Payment Date: _____
(Must be 14-27 days after Advance Date. If the First Regular Payment
Date is more than 14 days after the Advance Date an interest adjustment
amount will be required.)

☐ Semi-Monthly: Requested First Regular Payment Date: _____
(Must be at least 15 days, but less than 1 month after Advance Date. If the First Regular Payment Date is more
than 15 days after the Advance Date an interest adjustment amount will be required.)

☐ Monthly: Requested First Regular Payment Date: _____
(Must be at least 1 month, but less than 2 months after Advance Date. If the First Regular Payment Date is
more than 1 month after the Advance Date an interest adjustment amount will be required.)

☐ Check off if you elect to pay your own taxes.
(_____ reserves the right to ask for proof of up to date payment at any time.)

Your privilege of using any of the above payment frequencies may be cancelled should instalment arrears occur, or on breach of any covenants in the Mortgage or this Commitment Letter. If so, a monthly payment frequency will be reinstated. A Mid-Term Fee may be charged for changes made at any time after the Advance Date of the Mortgage.

     OR-030-031E   _____ _____ Borrower(s)/ Guarantor(s) Initials

SAMPLE: COMMITMENT
Monoline Cont'd

ADDITIONAL PROVISIONS FOR

1. EFFECT ON STANDARD TERMS:

These Additional Provisions form part of the Mortgage. In the event of any inconsistency or conflict between these Additional Provisions, the Commitment Letter, the Mortgage and the Standard Charge/ Mortgage Terms, the provisions of these documents shall apply in the following order of precedence to resolve the inconsistency or conflict: (i) the Commitment Letter; (ii) the Additional Provisions; (iii) the Mortgage; and (iv) the Standard Charge/Mortgage Terms.

2. CAPITALIZED TERMS:

All capitalized terms used but not otherwise defined in these Additional Provisions have the respective meanings ascribed to such terms in the Standard Charge/ Mortgage Terms.

3. INTEREST RATE:

We will charge you interest on the outstanding balance of your Mortgage at the Interest Rate from the Advance Date to the Interest Adjustment Date.

Starting on the Interest Adjustment Date, interest at the Interest Rate is compounded semi-annually, not in advance. For this purpose, we calculate interest for each payment period using a factor that is based on the Annual Interest Rate, compounded semi-annually. Interest is payable on the payment frequency selected by you (for example monthly). You promise to pay interest at the Interest Rate in effect at the time and as calculated above, on the outstanding balance of your Mortgage until paid in full.

Your Interest Rate is a Variable Interest Rate based on the Prime Rate and any applicable premium (or discount) to the Prime Rate as set out in the Mortgage. Based on this, the Interest Rate will change each time the Prime Rate changes, with no prior notice to you. Your Regularly Scheduled Payment will also change accordingly.

Compound Interest - If you do not pay interest when it is due, we will add the overdue interest to the outstanding balance of the Mortgage, and charge you interest on the combined amount until it is paid. This is called Compound Interest. We calculate Compound Interest at the current Annual Interest Rate in effect at the time. You promise to pay Compound Interest at the same frequency as the Regularly Scheduled Payments until the outstanding balance of the Mortgage, and any unpaid interest, is paid in full.

Interest at the Interest Rate will accrue and will be compounded in the same manner and is payable whether before or after default as well as prior to and after the Maturity Date on any Principal Amounts and on any unpaid interest outstanding from time to time. Interest whether before or after default as well as prior to and after the Maturity Date will accrue at the same rate as during the Term.

4. REGULARLY SCHEDULED PAYMENTS:

Your Regularly Scheduled Payment amount will change following a change in the Prime Rate. We recalculate your Regularly Scheduled Payment amount to an amount sufficient to pay the interest that will accrue to each Regularly Scheduled Payment date plus the amount of Principal that has to be paid to maintain the Amortization Period of the Mortgage. This amount will be your new Regularly Scheduled Payment amount until it is again changed following an increase or decrease in the Prime Rate. Any prepayments made by you will not affect your Regularly Scheduled Payments but will shorten your Amortization Period and will change the composition of interest and Principal in your Regularly Scheduled Payments.

If the amount of any Regularly Scheduled Payment is less than the accrued interest due over that payment period (ie. if the Prime Rate has increased over the payment period, but your rate adjustment has not yet been applied to your Mortgage), deferred interest will be added to the outstanding balance owing, and Compound Interest will apply.

5. PREPAYMENT PROVISIONS:

The following Prepayment Provisions are available to you each year of the Term of the Mortgage (i.e. during the 12 month period starting from the Interest Adjustment Date, and starting from each anniversary of the Interest Adjustment Date thereafter), provided you are not in default:

Borrower(s)/ Guarantor(s) Initials

SAMPLE: COMMITMENT
Monoline Cont'd

155

a) **Increased Payment**: Once per year, you may increase the amount of the Regularly Scheduled Payment up to a maximum of 20%. The maximum for each payment increase is calculated using the amount of the current Regularly Scheduled Payment in effect at the time.

b) **Lump Sum Payment**: You may make lump sum prepayments of $100 or more on any Regularly Scheduled Payment date, provided the total of these prepayments made throughout the year does not exceed 20% of the original Principal Amount.

If all or any portion of these privileges are not used in a particular year, they cannot be carried forward and used in a future year.

6.   EARLY PAYOUT PROVISIONS:

During the first 3 years of the Term:
- You may payout the entire outstanding balance of the Mortgage prior to the Maturity Date.
- If you exercise this option, a Reinvestment Fee and an Early Payout Penalty will apply.

In subsequent years of the Term (i.e. on or after the 3rd anniversary of the Interest Adjustment Date):
- You may payout the entire outstanding balance of the Mortgage, at any time.
- If you exercise this option, a Reinvestment Fee does not apply but an Early Payout Penalty will apply.

Reinvestment Fee:

The Reinvestment Fee is $500 in the first year of the Term, $400 in the second year, and $300 in the third year.   There is no Reinvestment Fee in subsequent years of the Term.

Early Payout Penalty:

The Early Payout Penalty is equal to 3 months simple interest.   This is calculated by applying your current Interest Rate in effect at the time OR the current Prime Rate in effect at the time as calculated (whichever is greater), to the outstanding Principal balance of your Mortgage, for a 3 month period.

If you request an Early Payout, you cannot exercise the lump sum and/or increased payment privileges (outlined in section 5a and 5b of this document), until the Payout Statement expires. The calculation of the Early Payout Penalty will be based on the outstanding Principal balance of your Mortgage.

7.   CONVERTIBILITY:

You may, at any time without penalty, convert this Variable Interest Rate Mortgage to an eligible closed fixed interest rate Mortgage offered by   at the time, provided that the new term plus the time elapsed on the existing Term is equal to or greater than the original Term.   You may select from the options available at the time of conversion.   You will receive the interest rate we quote at the time, for the term selected. You will sign a Renewal Agreement which will contain all of the amended terms and conditions of the new Mortgage. All the features and benefits of the existing Mortgage are amended upon conversion, and you will adopt the features and benefits of the new Mortgage. You cannot convert if you are in default.

8.   RENEWAL:

The outstanding balance of the Mortgage is due and payable on the Maturity Date; however, we may offer to renew it prior to the Maturity Date. If we have sent you a Renewal Agreement (in advance of the Maturity Date), and:

i.   If you accept the Renewal Agreement:
All the features and benefits of the existing Mortgage are amended upon renewal, and you will adopt the features and benefits of the new Mortgage.

ii.   If you fail to either accept or decline the Renewal Agreement, and do not pay out the Mortgage on the Maturity Date:
   a. **The Mortgage will automatically renew into a 6 Month Convertible closed term Mortgage on the Maturity Date.**
   b. The renewed 6 Month Convertible closed term Mortgage will provide you with the option to subsequently convert it to a longer closed term, fixed rate Mortgage without penalty, at any time during the renewal term.
   c. If you choose to pay out the outstanding balance of your 6 Month Convertible Mortgage during the renewal term, you will be subject to the Early Payout Penalty (which is the greater of the Interest Rate Differential Amount or Three Months Interest Cost), plus a Reinvestment Fee.

You may not renew your Mortgage prior to the end of your Term.   However, if you wish to switch to a new Term prior to the Maturity Date, you can do so upon payment of any penalties or fees associated with Early Payouts.

9.   ASSUMABILITY:

Borrower(s)/ Guarantor(s) Initials

SAMPLE: COMMITMENT
Monoline Cont'd

This Mortgage is assumable subject   s consent. For details, refer to the Standard Charge/ Mortgage Terms.

10. PORTABILITY:

This Mortgage is portable subject to   : consent. For details, refer to the Standard Charge/ Mortgage Terms.

156

11. SKIP-A-PAYMENT:

This Mortgage does not permit skip-a-payment.

12. ASSIGNMENT BY   :

Without the consent of, and without notice to, the Borrowers and Guarantors, and without affecting the Obligations of the Borrowers and Guarantors under this Mortgage,   may assign, transfer, sell, pledge or convey this Commitment Letter (prior to and after any Advances), this Mortgage, or any portion of this Mortgage to any third party ("Third Party") in relation to a sale, securitization, financing, pledging or security arrangement. The Borrowers and Guarantors agree, and for this purpose grant ! an irrevocable power of attorney coupled with an interest, to execute and register in any applicable land titles or registry office any and all documentation, notices and agreements required to evidence or perfect any assignment, transfer, sale, pledge, conveyance or security arrangement pursuant to this Section. On any notice of an assignment, transfer, sale, pledge, conveyance or security arrangement pursuant to this Section from   or from a Third Party (as consented to by   ), the Borrowers and Guarantors shall make all payments due under this Mortgage to such Third Party as mortgagee hereunder.

Borrower(s)/ Guarantor(s) Initials

SAMPLE: COMMITMENT
B Lender

MORTGAGE COMMITMENT

B LENDER	Underwriter		Date
	Mortgage Reference Number:		
	Deal Number:		

We are pleased to confirm that your application for a Mortgage Loan has been approved under the following terms and conditions:

BORROWER(S):	PURPOSE: Purchase
Covenantor(S):	
SECURITY ADDRESS:	LEGAL DESCRIPTION:

COMMITMENT DATE:	COMMITMENT EXPIRY DATE:	ADVANCE DATE:
INTEREST ADJUSTMENT DATE:	FIRST PAYMENT DATE:	MATURITY DATE:

LOAN TYPE:		LTV:	65.00%
BASIC LOAN AMOUNT:		INTEREST RATE:	4.890%
MTG.INSUR.PREMIUM:	$0.00	TERM:	2 years 0 months Closed
TOTAL LOAN AMOUNT:	$471,250.00	AMORTIZATION PERIOD:	30 years 0 months
PST ON INSUR.PREMIUM:	$0.00	PAYMENT FREQUENCY:	Monthly
BASIC PAYMENT AMOUNT:	$2,484.15	TAXES TO BE PAID BY:	Borrower
EST.ANNUAL PROP.TAXES:	$2,169.00		
MORTGAGE FEES:			
Processing Fee (Take From First Advance)		$7,068.75	

TERMS AND CONDITIONS

All of our standard requirements and, if applicable, those of the mortgage insurer must be met. All costs, including legal, survey, mortgage insurance etc. are for the account of the borrower(s). The mortgage insurance premium (if applicable) will be added to the basic loan amount. Any fees specified herein may be deducted from the Mortgage advance. If for any reason the loan is not advanced, you agree to pay all application, legal, appraisal and survey costs incurred in this transaction.

This Mortgage Commitment is subject to the details, terms and conditions outlined herein. No deletions from or additions to the Mortgage are permissible unless approved by

This mortgage will be subject to the extended terms in   standard mortgage form and Standard Charge Mortgage Terms. (Applicant)

THIS COMMITMENT IS CONDITIONAL UPON RECEIPT OF THE FOLLOWING

The following conditions must be met, and the requested documents must be received in form and content satisfactory to no later than five (5) days prior to the advance of the mortgage. Failure to do so may delay or void this commitment.

1.   (A) Receipt of a gift letter showing the amount of the gift $253,750.00 and confirming that the gift is not repayable. The letter must be dated and signed by both the donor and the recipient.
B) The gift must be verified as being in the applicant's bank account no less than 15 days prior to the funding date, by a bank statement showing the applicant's name, account number and corresponding deposit amount.
C) Ability to Gift *Ability to gift has been received* (Applicant)

2.   This commitment is subject to the submitting broker providing   with the following: (1) Name of the main broker the application is submitted under (2) Your full contact information including phone number, email address and address (3) Your license number including all the provinces you are licensed in. For further information please contact your local BDM. Thank you. (Underwriter)

SAMPLE: COMMITMENT
B Lender Cont'd

3. A Pre-Authorized Payment authorization (Form #4503) completed and signed by the client and accompanied with a personalized VOID cheque or form stamped by the financial institution confirming account ownership is required. (Solicitor)

4. Confirmation that the following debts have been paid in full prior to closing:
   BELL MOBILITY debt of $202.00,
   ROGERS SB WESTERN 2 WIRELESS debt of $632.00,
   AB HEALTH SERVICES debt of $260.00,
   AB HEALTH SERVICES debt of $260.00,
   SHAW CABLESYSTEMS G P IV debt of $1,236.00,
   KEYSTONE FINANCE debt of $9,789.00,
   TD AUTO FINANCE CAN debt of $10,000.00,
   TELUS MOBILITY debt of $697.00,
   EASYFINANCIAL debt of $3,731.00,
   TDCT debt of $61,000.00,

   (Solicitor)

5. requires copy of Title/Deed confirming all parties on Offer to Purchase are currently on Title/Deed. If Title/Deed is in corporate name, a copy of the Articles of Incorporation is required to confirm signing authorities. (Solicitor)

6. will require satisfactory confirmation that the applicants are on the TIPPS program where offered. (Solicitor)

7. requires Title Insurance (Solicitor)

8. A Lender Processing Fee of $7068.75 will be deducted from the mortgage proceeds at time of closing.

   (Solicitor)

9. Statutory declaration signed by mortgagor(s) indicating that the property will be owner occupied. (Solicitor)

10. You will be required to sign a mortgage disclosure statement in accordance with the consumer protection legislation of your Province. This statement will be signed at your solicitor's office at the time the mortgage document is signed. (Solicitor)

11. PREPAYMENT PRIVILEGES
    Each year, on the Anniversary Date of your mortgage only, you may make a lump sum payment of up to 20% of the principal amount owing on the mortgage at the beginning of your current term without paying a penalty or charge. Prepayments requested at any other time are not allowed. The total value cannot be more than 20% of the original principal amount without paying a penalty or charge and must be at least $500.00. Even though you may have prepaid less than 20% of the principal amount on previous Anniversary Dates, the prepayment privilege amount does not carry forward.
    Prepayment privileges are not available on one year Terms.
    PREPAYMENT CHARGES
    If you want to payout your mortgage in full, or if you want to make a payment in an amount greater than your available Prepayment Privilege (which can only be done on the Anniversary Date of your mortgage), the amount being prepaid will be subject to a Prepayment Charge calculated as follows:
    a) If your Prepayment is made at any time in the first year of your Term, up to and including the first Anniversary Date, you will pay a Prepayment Charge of 3% of the amount being prepaid.
    b) If your Prepayment is made after your first Anniversary Date, up to and including your second Anniversary Date, you will pay a Prepayment Charge of 2% of the amount being prepaid.
    c) If your Prepayment is made any time after your second Anniversary Date, but before your Maturity Date, you will pay a Prepayment Charge of 1% of the amount being prepaid
    *Prepayments made on the Anniversary Date will be calculated by reducing the amount being prepaid by the allowable Prepayment Privilege amount.
    If you have any questions regarding Prepayment Charges please contact us at (Solicitor)

12. will refuse any subsequent financial charges to be registered against the subject property without Bank's approval

    British Columbia, (Solicitor)

13. requires satisfactory written confirmation of employment at , form of letter on Company letterhead reflecting: (i) Start date, (ii) Position, (iii) Minimum annual salary $64,064.00 supported with a current pay stub. The information will be verified by prior to funding. If Applicant(s) are not salaried, further conditions will apply. (Broker)

14. must receive a fully executed Agreement of Purchase and Sale along with MLS Listing for the property being purchased. Documents must be deemed satisfactory to Agreement should include the vendors full name, address and phone number, realtor information. Property information to include sq. footage, heat type, garage type and size.

SAMPLE: COMMITMENT
B Lender Cont'd

(Broker)

15. Please provide confirmation of current ownership by way of copy of Title or current property tax assessment. (Broker)

16. FOR AMENDMENTS PLEASE EMAIL:

17. The interest rate quoted on this mortgage approval is valid for a period of up to (90) sixty days or until the funding date, whichever occurs first. In the event that funds have not been advanced for any reason within this period,   reserves the right to adjust the interest rate and/or terms and conditions. The rate on this commitment will expire .   (Broker)

18.   to obtain a full 12 months of bank statements in good standing confirming existing mortgage/alternate trades have paid as agreed for a minimum of 12 months (Broker)

19. Please provide the entitlement letter to confirm   (Broker)

20.   requires confirmation of property taxes of $ /yr. (Broker)

21. Vendor and purchaser CANNOT use same solicitor or office. (Broker)

22. We require a full Appraisal report for the subject property, addressed to   and completed by a approved appraiser. Appraisal costs are the borrowers responsibility. Appraisal report to confirm property condition as average or better, prime and marketable within 120 days, and a minimum value of 725k   reserves the right to decline or amend the commitment based upon our review of the appraisal and suitability of the security. Appraisal can include home, garage and 10 acres, no outbuildings. No aspect of the home can come back in fair condition. Please order through one of the following:

(Broker)

23. Please provide written confirmation that the Telus 02 has been paid up to date (Broker)

24. Signed Commitment (Broker)

25. Solicitor Name and Address (Broker)

Requests for any changes to the terms and conditions of the Commitment will only be considered if your request is received by us in writing at least 5 business days prior to the Advance Date.

This Commitment is open for acceptance by you until 11:59 pm   at which time, if not accepted, will be null and void. Furthermore, the mortgage must be advanced by   at which time if not advanced or extended, it expires.

Authorized by: _____

PERSONAL INFORMATION AND PRIVACY

             respects the privacy of our customers and is committed to protecting the personal information you provide to us. We will use your personal information only for the purposes for which it was collected, as permitted under applicable laws and for purposes for which you have provided your consent

Notice and Consent regarding Personal Information. By signing the acknowledgement, waiver and consent below, you acknowledge that you have been given notice of and you consent to:

- verification by   of your personal information with any credit reporting agency, creditor, financial institution, your employer, or any other person with whom you may have financial dealings You hereby authorize those persons to disclose your personal information to us for this purpose;

- disclosure of your personal information to   affiliates, agents, mortgage investors and service providers and their successors and assigns for purposes of the administration of mortgages and related services;

- disclosure of your personal information to mortgage insurers, including CMHC, Genworth and Canada Guaranty for mortgage default insurance purposes; and

SAMPLE: COMMITMENT
B Lender Cont'd

160

• _____ "_____" _____ and its affiliates may use your personal information to assess your initial and ongoing creditworthiness for your mortgage, for ongoing servicing of your mortgage account and to determine your eligibility for other credit products and services such as a credit card.

In addition, from time to time, we may disclose personal information we collect to allow, our agents, affiliates, third parties and other selected companies to promote products and services to you that may be of benefit or interest to you. The information we may disclose to them will contain general information such as names, addresses and telephone numbers and categories of goods and services reflecting your interests and preferences. In no case will sensitive information, including specific financial data or credit ratings be disclosed to third parties for purposes of promoting products and services without your express consent. If you prefer that we not share your personal information with third parties for these purposes, you may opt out at any time by calling us toll free at

Acceptance:

I / We _____ warrant that all representations made by me/us and all the information submitted to you in connection with my/our mortgage application are true and accurate. I / We fully understand that any misrepresentations of fact contained in my/our mortgage application or other documentation entitles you to decline to advance a portion or all of the loan, or to demand immediate repayment of all monies secured by the Mortgage.

I / We, the undersigned Borrowers and Covenantors (if applicable) accept the terms of this Mortgage Commitment and agree to fulfill the conditions of approval outlined herein.

_____ _____ _____
WITNESS   BORROWER   DATE

_____ _____ _____
WITNESS   CO-BORROWER   DATE

_____ _____ _____
WITNESS   COVENANTOR   DATE

SAMPLE: COMMITMENT
Private Lender

Date Commitment Issued:

We hereby offer you mortgage financing with the following terms:

Subject to: (1) Lender Inspection
(2) Satisfactory Appraisal (Lender Approved)
(3) Strata Form B
(4) Depreciation Report (if available)

Mortgagor(s) / Borrower(s):
(1)
(2)
(3)
(4)

Covenantor(s) / Guarantor(s):
(1)
(2)

Property to be Mortgaged:
A.
B.
C.
D.

Mortgage Charge(s):

Our Charge over Property A: 2nd   Our Charge over Property B: N/A
Our Charge over Property C: N/A   Our Charge over Property D: N/A

Type(s) Of Charge: Face Value of Loan: $ 40,000.00
Line Of Credit / . / .   1st Advance: $ tbd by borrower

Payments: $ 332.00 Per Month (Interest Only)   Interest Rate: 9.95%
Based on Face Value advanced   Compounded Monthly, not in advance

Mortgage Term:
1 YEAR – OPEN (can be paid out or paid down at any time - without penalty)

Prior Charges:					
Property A:		Property B:		Property C:	
Amount	Lender	Amount	Lender	Amount	Lender
1st $ 154,000	First National	1st		1st	
2nd $		2nd		2nd	
3rd $		3rd		3rd	

Page 1 of 2

SAMPLE: COMMITMENT
Private Lender Cont'd

162

- **Fee for arranging financing:** The borrower shall pay to   Inc.
  a fee in the amount of $ 2,000.00 for arranging financing. This fee shall be deemed to
  have been earned by   upon execution of this agreement by the borrower, as
  compensation for the time, effort and expense incurred by   with respect to the
  financing contemplated herein.

- **Fee to the Lender:** $ 0.00

- **Inspection/Commitment Deposit: $1,000.00 By Money Order / Cash -**
  To cover costs incurred on your behalf, balance credited to your mortgage account with
  the lender. If lender inspection occurs and funding doesn't proceed for any reason,
  deposit is earned as inspection fee and arrangement fee, noted above, is due and payable.

- **Conditions:** Throughout the term, the lender requires that all payments be made as
  agreed (includes mortgage, property taxes, strata fees etc.) Fire insurance must be in
  place at all times (up to the cost of replacement value of the improvements). At the time
  of funding, you will be required to sign our Pre-Authorized Debit (PAD) Agreement and
  provide us with a "Void" cheque. Monthly payments will be automatically debited on the
  1st day (or first business day) of the month from your designated bank account for the
  monthly payments. There is a $100 charge for NSF cheques or non-payments. The
  mortgage is not assumable. The above funds may be provided by a source not dealing at
  arm's length with   Inc.

- **Legal Costs:** The mortgage will be prepared by   for the lender.
  The borrower is responsible for the legal costs incurred. The borrower has the option
  to sign the prepared documents in the presence of their own lawyer/notary.

This commitment must be signed by the mortgagor(s) and guarantor(s) and must be received in
our office (by fax, original or photocopy) by   It will remain in effect for
ten days from the acceptance date.

Mortgagor's/Guarantor's Acceptance
(By signing this, you agree to all the terms and conditions stated above in this commitment):

_____
Borrower #1

_____
Borrower #2 or Guarantor

_____
Borrower #3 or Guarantor

_____
Borrower #4 or Guarantor

_____ Acceptance Date

COMPLIANCE

Any documents that must be completed and signed by borrowers to comply with government rules and regulations are usually provided at the same time as the lender's commitment.

Compliance documents can vary from province to province. In BC, they include:

Mortgage Life & Disability Insurance Review

Your broker is required to verify that you have adequate coverage in place and are aware of your insurance options.

BC Cost of Credit Disclosure

This is a summary that sets out a brief description of the loan and the costs associated with borrowing. It factors in the estimated **closing costs**, such as legal fees, title insurance (to be discussed in Chapter 11) and appraisal fees. A new annual percentage rate (APR), inclusive of these costs, is provided. In addition to the cost of credit disclosure form provided by the mortgage broker, each lender provides their disclosure statement as well. The solicitor will be instructed to present it to you and review it with you before you sign.

BC Form 10 Conflict of Interest Disclosure

In most cases, the lender pays your broker a finder's fee for arranging your mortgage.

Form 10 advises that finder's fee payment comes from the lender and not from the borrower. The commissions documented, including any volume, efficiency or marketing bonuses, are the *maximum* that could be collected by the **mortgage brokerage**, not necessarily the amount that will be collected.

Finder's fees vary based on the lender, term, type of mortgage, the volume of mortgages referred by the broker or brokerage, efficiency practices and special offerings. In today's market, a brokerage is usually paid between 0.5% and 1% of the mortgage amount. For example, a $400,000 mortgage will yield gross commissions of $2,000 to $4,000 as a finder's fee. The brokerage then pays the **sub-mortgage broker** a portion of the fee based on their contract split. Less common in the industry are brokerages that operate with a flat monthly fee model, where a broker pays a set amount each month and receives 100% of finder's fees.

Form 10 also requires the broker to disclose any interest in the property if this exists.

IMPORTANT! If financing is arranged from a B lender (alternative lender), private lender or for construction or commercial financing, you are responsible for any fees required to arrange the mortgage. The fees vary depending on the amount and nature of the financing required. The fees will be detailed along with the mortgage commitment so you know and understand the costs before proceeding.

Client Consent

Monoline lenders usually offer a client consent form that can be included in the compliance package. If signed, it allows your broker to act on your behalf to inquire about or address issues of concern related to your tax account, payments or penalties, etc. It can be a huge timesaver to have the mortgage broker act as your advocate. You can request to remove any third-party consent from your account at any time.

Solicitor/Realtor Authorization

Some brokers provide an authorization form to allow them to release information to other members of your real estate team. This can help ensure everyone is connected and working together effectively and efficiently to get the process completed.

LINGO!

SUB-MORTGAGE BROKER

An individual mortgage broker, like me. While I'm an independent business owner, being associated with a brokerage allows me to effectively and efficiently process mortgage applications.

CLOSING COSTS

These are costs that can be incurred when purchasing a home, refinancing or switching your mortgage. They include legal fees, transfer fees, disbursements, **property transfer tax (PTT)** and inspector and appraisal costs. These are in addition to the down payment. Lenders usually request that a borrower prove they have 1.5% of the purchase price available for closing costs, in addition to the down payment. Exceptions can be made for first-time homebuyers, who are not required to pay PTT. See Chapter 12 for a full breakdown of closing costs.

PROPERTY TRANSFER TAX (LAND TRANSFER TAX)

A tax charged by many provinces and municipalities that buyers must pay upon closing, usually a percentage of the purchase price. In BC, the tax is 1% on the first $200,000, 2% on the portion greater than $200,000 up to and including $2,000,000 and 3% on the portion greater than $3,000,000. This tax can be waived for first-time homebuyers purchasing a property under $500,000 or for all buyers purchasing new builds under $750,000.

Other provinces have other land transfer tax schedules; provinces such as Alberta and Saskatchewan have smaller land title transfer fees.

MORTGAGE BROKERAGE

A mortgage company (in some cases a franchise) that manages sub-mortgage brokers to complete mortgage financing.

CONDITIONS SATISFIED

Once all the conditions required by the mortgage commitment have been satisfied and approved by the lender, you have removed all subjects on your offer and the compliance documents are complete, the file will be sent to the lender branch or your solicitor's office to be prepared for your official legal signing.

YOUR TEAM

Mortgage Broker

They will provide and explain the mortgage commitment and compliance documents and manage the process to ensure conditions requested by the lender are met and approved by the subject removal date. If an appraisal is required, they will order it through a lender-approved source. Your broker will also advise when all the conditions of the commitment have been met so you can remove the subjects on your offer and proceed with the purchase.

Home Insurance Broker

They will help you find the right home insurance policy (in particular, fire insurance) for your property. It must be active on the possession date. Some lenders may also require earthquake insurance. Your insurer's contact details will need to be provided to your solicitor. Some brokers may provide referral options along with your mortgage commitment and compliance package.

Insurance Broker/Financial Planner

They can help ensure that you and your family are protected with the right life and disability coverage. Adding a property and mortgage to your portfolio is a significant financial change. Life has a way of throwing obstacles in our way, and if you or your family can't pay the mortgage, your home and dreams could be lost.

Through an insurance broker and/or a financial planner who provides insurance products as part of their portfolio of services, clients have access to a choice of policies from a variety of different insurance companies—similar to working with a mortgage broker. These policies could provide lump-sum benefits that are not tied specifically to paying off your mortgage. Investigating insurance options early on is important. In many cases, it can take months before coverage is initiated.

If you do not have an insurance policy large enough to cover your new mortgage payments and are planning to source insurance options through a broker later, it's worth considering a policy that is offered with your mortgage to ensure you are protected immediately. If you find a better option later, the policy can be cancelled.

STEP 1	**STEP 2**	**STEP 3**	**STEP 4**	**STEP 5**
Application	Search/Submit	Commitment	Instructed	Completion

STEP 4: INSTRUCTED

Once all mortgage commitment conditions are met, the lender will "instruct" the file to the approved solicitor to complete your legal signing and title registration.

With this instruction, the lender is guiding the solicitor to complete the mortgage and registration in accordance with the lender's requirements. Debts may need to be paid out, special documentation may need to be verified or additional requests such as proof of independent legal advice (if a spouse is not on the mortgage and title of the property) may have to be met.

ONE OR TWO APPOINTMENTS

The legal signing finalizes the purchase, refinance or switch/transfer, the title is transferred and the mortgage is registered. Depending on the mortgage lender, the signing will be complete in one or two steps:

168

ONE STEP: MONOLINE & PRIVATE LENDERS; SOME BANKS	TWO STEPS: CREDIT UNIONS & SCOTIABANK
Only require the signing with the solicitor or a third-party legal provider such as First Canadian Title (FCT) or Fidelity National Financial Canada (FNF).	A branch signing before the solicitor signing is required. Other lender products will be offered at this time. Credit unions will also require borrowers to become members for a small fee. If a third-party provider such as FCT or FNF is used, the representative is usually made available at the branch signing to complete in one visit.
	Once branch signing is complete, the borrower meets with the solicitor to complete registration.

FCT AND FNF

In addition to providing services such as title insurance, FCT and FNF provide legal services for lenders to complete special refinance and switch programs at a reduced rate.

TIMING YOUR SOLICITOR MEETING

The meeting with your solicitor should ideally be set up at least three days before the closing date to allow time to resolve any issues and prepare for fund transfer. More lead time is even better; however, market conditions dictate the availability of solicitors, and so it is not always an option.

STATEMENT OF ADJUSTMENTS (SOA)

The solicitor will provide a statement of adjustments before or at your meeting. It will advise how much, if any, additional funds will be required to complete the purchase or if a surplus of funds remains from a refinance.

For a purchase, the SOA will include the property tax and strata fees adjusted between the seller and buyer, property transfer tax owed, the deposits paid, mortgage proceeds from the lender and the costs associated with the legal transaction. If outstanding funds are owed, these are to be provided by the buyer by way of a bank draft. Some solicitors now accept e-transfers. For a sample of an SOA, see page 87.

For a refinance or switch/transfer, the SOA will adjust the fees and costs of closing the previous mortgage, any debts paid and legal fees. If a balance is owing, the borrower will be required to provide a bank draft or e-transfer to the solicitor; any excess funds will be released to the borrower by direct deposit or bank draft.

CHECKING THE NUMBERS

If your broker has not provided you with a release document that allows your solicitor to send him or her the SOA directly, it's a good idea for you to forward a copy for review. Many hands touch a mortgage commitment before it reaches the solicitor. Human error does happen. Bring a copy of your mortgage commitment or have an electronic copy available on your phone so you can cross-reference the numbers. If something looks incorrect, contact your mortgage broker immediately.

TRANSFER OF TITLE/MORTGAGE REGISTRATION

The solicitor will provide you with a signed copy of the mortgage documents. A title transfer of ownership or the new title (for refinance/switch/transfer) with a new mortgage registration will be provided once it is completed by the land title office. This may take a few weeks.

Be sure to review and confirm that the old charges have been removed and the correct mortgage charge remains. Again, errors happen.

YOUR TEAM

Solicitor

A lawyer or notary completes the title registration of the property and mortgage, the final and most important detail in the purchase and sale transaction. A lawyer and notary provide the same services of:

1. Conducting a title search to confirm property is purchased from the rightful owner and is free of all charges and liens;
2. Obtaining tax information;

3. Preparing a SOA that details how much money needs to be transferred between the buyer and the seller.

4. Preparing closing documents, including the title transfer, mortgage and property transfer tax forms, and communicating with the seller's solicitor for execution.

170

WHAT ARE THE KEY DIFFERENCES BETWEEN A LAWYER AND A NOTARY PUBLIC?	
LAWYER	**NOTARY**
Can represent you in disputes and in court;	Cannot represent you in disputes or court;
Can provide legal advice;	Focuses only on non-contentious issues such as real estate, estate planning and other documentation. They only have the legal power to register and sign off on documents.
Carries professional liability insurance; and	Carries professional liability insurance; and
Has a law degree and has been accepted as a member of their provincial law society.	Has an undergraduate degree and has completed the BC Notaries Course through the University of British Columbia or provincial equivalent.

Mortgage Broker

They will verify that instructions have been received by the solicitor. Experienced brokers will usually have strong partnerships with expert real estate law offices in the region to ensure clear communication and important details aren't missed. If location allows, my practice is to provide a solicitor referral source with the mortgage commitment and compliance package.

STEP 1
Application

STEP 2
Search/Submit

STEP 3
Commitment

STEP 4
Instructed

STEP 5
Completion

STEP 5: COMPLETION OF NEW HOME OR NEW MORTGAGE

171

On completion day, your realtor usually has the pleasure of handing you the keys to your new home. You can move in or prepare it for whatever purpose it was purchased—it's yours.

If you have completed a refinance or a switch/transfer to a new lender, your new mortgage will commence.

PAYMENTS BEGIN

Following completion, most lenders send out a welcome package and mortgage overview. If the lender has an online client portal, which is usually the case with monoline lenders, you'll be given the details so you can manage your mortgage online.

As mentioned before, First National has one of the best client portals in the industry. Many monoline lenders have expanded their portals to be very competitive as well. To get a sampling of the power behind these customer portals, view First National's My Mortgage Portal by *googling: First National my mortgage demo.*

ANNUAL STATEMENTS

By law, you should receive at least one mortgage statement each year from your lender. If you require any updated details, you can always contact your customer service support or, if you have an online portal, refer to that.

A list of our most popular lender customer service contacts and client portal websites is available at the end of this book.

PROPERTY TAXES

Each year in BC, homeowners must claim their Home Owner's Grant (HOG) of $570 towards their property tax bill. The grant is available only for owner-occupied units; rental and other investment properties do not qualify. Seniors and persons living with a disability and rural locations may also be eligible for further grants.

172

Homeowners must register for the grant each and every year, or they may forfeit the opportunity. Registration can be completed by filling out and mailing the grant portion on the property tax notice or online on the municipal website. *Google your municipal name + home owner grant.* You will need the folio number and access code from your property tax notice. Your online registration can be completed in seconds.

I send a reminder email to all my clients to claim their HOG each year: I don't want anyone to miss out on the annual savings!

ANNIVERSARY CHECK-UP

Some mortgage brokers do an annual mortgage review to ensure their clients are maximizing their mortgage savings. Whether this service is offered or not, it's worth checking in with your mortgage broker at least once a year to ensure you are in the best product for your current needs. Life can throw us for loops, and knowing where you stand with your mortgage and investment can be invaluable to future financial decisions. As mentioned earlier, if there is ever a time of hardship or divorce, it is best to contact your mortgage broker immediately. There may be options that can help ease the pressures that otherwise have the potential to cost thousands of dollars or permanently impact your credit.

BANK OF CANADA OVERNIGHT RATE TARGET ANNOUNCEMENTS

The Bank of Canada announces its key policy interest rate (overnight target rate) eight times a year. A calendar of the scheduled announcements is available by *googling: BOC overnight rate announcement.*

These announcements have the potential to impact variable-rate borrowers through changes to lender's prime rates. Your broker may email or call to advise of any updates and if it will mean any change to your mortgage or payment.

Between September 2010 and 2017, borrowers experienced a largely stable overnight rate and benefited from two 0.25% decreases in 2015—lenders only dropped their prime rates by 0.15%.

July 2017 was the first increase in the overnight rate in seven years. September 2017 brought a shocking consecutive increase. The back-to-back quarter point (0.25%) increases were matched by the lenders. A third 0.25% increase was announced in January 2018. There is widespread speculation that increases may continue intermittently over the next few years.

You can refer to the Bank of Canada Overnight Rate announcements chart showing changes since 2006 on page 98.

YOUR TEAM

Mortgage Broker

Your broker is available for any follow-up questions or concerns about your mortgage. He or she should be your first point of contact if you have a question regarding your mortgage or you are considering changes. Sometimes the broker may not be able to assist with making the changes, but they can direct you to the right contact to make the process more efficient.

Use your mortgage broker as a resource and advocate. An annual review is important to ensure you are making the most out of your mortgage investment.

QUESTIONS?

We've covered a whole lot of ground at a time you probably just want to think about marble countertops, square footage and maybe a little bistro patio. It's hard to digest, I know. That's why I'm here.

Use the space below to jot down some initial questions for your next conversation with your mortgage broker. What aren't you quite clear on? Credit, income, down payment, product options or property type and use? Is there anything else you'd like to know about the application process?

CHAPTER 9
Living the Life on Richards

S hortly after our wedding, Mark's best man (and best friend) forwarded a job posting he thought might interest me. It did. With big eyes, I applied and was hired. A "Pinch me!" moment.

I moved from one of the smallest companies associated with the Olympic Games to one of the largest, in fact, the largest for the Winter Games. It made for a better commute initially, but the plan was for me to move from downtown Vancouver to New Westminster. If you know the lower mainland, and especially the transit system, you'll understand that commuting from Richmond to New Westminster (before the Canada Line) with no car is pretty close to impossible— or at least extremely painful. I was screaming, "NO WAY!"

I immediately initiated joint purchase number two; ownership of property number three, in downtown Vancouver.

We looked at refinancing the Oxford property to help with this initiative but found the penalties too high to justify the amount we'd be able to access.

178 Instead, we rolled the mortgage into a "Homeline Plan" so that we would keep the mortgage amount but also get a home equity line of credit for the additional equity available in the property. To this day, I am not sure how we qualified for this, but my guess is that it was simply the fact that the rules were much different then.

Out I went, without Mark, as it was high season in the golf industry. Saturdays were his busiest day, and Saturdays were also when all the open houses were scheduled. Our realtor and I went on an open-house shopping spree, and by the end of the day, we were making an offer on a property on Richards Street that Mark hadn't even seen.

In July of 2009, we became the owners of our third condo in the lower mainland. Crazy! One rental in East Van (655 square feet), one rental in Richmond (915 square feet) and our owner-occupied, cozy (630 square feet) one-bedroom with den in downtown Vancouver. (Its primary claim to fame was winning a design award for Vancouver's "sexiest bathroom.") Our mortgage was arranged by our trusted mortgage broker: a five-year fixed-term, 35-year amortization, at 3.79%.

We lived it, we loved it, and we want to go back. It was the perfect time to live in downtown Vancouver, which was lively and full of spirit. We loved that we could work all day or night, come home and, at 11 p.m., still be able to head downstairs to grab milk, bread, tomatoes and mayo. Or better yet, order sushi, walk to pick it up and be back to eat it in less than 10 minutes. We were also in the perfect spot for getting in and out of the city quickly, wherever we needed to go. It worked well for both of our jobs, and it was close to everything, including shops, transit, restaurants—and St. Paul's Hospital, which we walked to while in labour with our firstborn. Yes, things changed again.

One random day I reconnected with a long-time university friend. As part of catching up on our lives, I told him I felt challenged trying to figure out what to do next if I didn't continue in the Olympics. He was working as a mortgage specialist in Calgary and said he thought it was something that would really fit with my personality and work ethic.

He and I had gone to school together, worked together, campaigned together and lived together, so he had a pretty good read on the type of person I am. His idea lodged in the back of my mind.

While I could continue with the Olympics, I was also ready to start nesting. In the days leading up to the 2010 Games in Vancouver, Mark and I decided to start our family.

With a baby on the way and my contract ending, I needed to start looking for a new job immediately. Trouble was, it seemed like everyone and their dog were looking for a job too. The 2010 Olympics were over, and thousands of people who had left their permanent jobs to work on the Games now needed a new one. My three-games history meant nothing to a business or recruiter. Fear was setting in, and pregnancy was taking a toll. My "morning sickness" lasted all day long, and it was all I could do to get through the day, let alone ramp up my efforts to find employment.

After a couple of months of living like a couch potato and smelling like a teenager's hockey bag, too lazy and sick to grab water when I was thirsty, sometimes not even showering for five days at a time, I finally started feeling like I might have passed the lowest point. I felt better and more mobile. I could finally eat, walk and breathe. I had the energy to lift my hands over my head to wash my hair. But now, I needed to find a job.

With my love of real estate investment, it just felt right to become a mortgage broker. I decided to take the courses I needed while I was on maternity leave so I could launch my business when our baby was a year old. To help pay our mortgages in the meantime, I got a short-term gig as a temporary catering manager for one of the most prestigious private golf clubs in BC.

As my due date rolled closer, we had some other personal business to deal with too. We were still living in a one-bedroom apartment, with a baby on the way. We had many discussions with our realtor and mortgage broker. We considered how long we could live there with the three of us and then considered all our other options. Should we sell the one-bedroom downtown and move closer to the golf club where Mark and I were now both working? Could we keep the downtown unit if we moved somewhere else? What could we buy if we sold both the Richmond and Oxford properties?

We started with a plan to buy a townhouse in Port Moody, an area we liked. But the townhouses we saw there never seemed right. Or, if we liked it, it was too tight financially. It was exhausting—tons of open houses. We expanded our search to other communities such as Coquitlam, Pitt Meadows and even to Walnut Grove in Surrey. It felt more like work, and there was much more disappointment than excitement.

We finally found a property we were ready to make an offer on, but the allowable rental income that would come from our three other properties was limiting us on the offer we could make. It was a 20th-floor unit in Port Moody for $412,000. Inventory was high at the time, and we found out the seller had to sell, so odds were good we would get it, but it was not meant to be. Our numbers weren't meshing with all the properties on the books, not to mention my pending maternity leave.

Then our search had to stop. It was baby time.

With a baby to look after, our son Jack, we eventually made what seemed like the safest decision, to sell the Richards property and move back to our place in Richmond. It was a hard choice to make and one I regret to this day. Looking back with mortgage broker expertise, 20/20 vision of the market, and less emotional attachment, selling Oxford and keeping Richards or keeping all three properties and renting ourselves would have been better choices.

Yet the decision to move to Richmond instead of towards Port Moody ended up being a blessing in disguise.

Now you ....

Was there a time when you faced bleak prospects and worried you might not be able to cover your expenses—including, perhaps, your mortgage or rent?

What were the primary lessons you learned from that experience?

182

Has there been a time you regretted making the "safe" decision? Or a time you took a risk that didn't work out? If so, what was the cost? Have these experiences changed the way you make decisions, and if so, how?

CHAPTER 10

Own and Save with Mortgage and Home Programs

There are many mortgage programs that help Canadians access the financing they need for homeownership. This is not an exhaustive list, but it highlights some of the more popular options available today through the government and insurers as well as some unique options from some of our lenders. As with most things in the mortgage industry, these programs are subject to change or can be discontinued at any time.

B2B EQUITY 50 OR EQUITY 65

If clients prefer to keep proof-of-income paperwork to a minimum or have elevated debt-servicing ratios and a down payment or equity of 35% or greater, they may be able to purchase or refinance a marketable **owner-occupied property** with B2B's Equity 50 or Equity 65 program.

For more information:

Google: B2B Equity 50

LINGO!

OWNER-OCCUPIED PROPERTY

A property purchased as a principal residence or second home. This can include a home with secondary suites used for rental. This type of purchase can be made with as little as a 5% down payment, whether you are a first-time home-buyer or not.

Mortgages on owner-occupied properties typically have better rates than those on properties purchased for investment purposes. The down payment requirement can be as little as 2.5% in BC if you are a first-time homebuyer taking advantage of the BC HOME Partnership program.

BC HOME PARTNERSHIP PROGRAM

BC Home Owner Mortgage and Equity Partnership (BC HOME Partnership) assists residents of British Columbia who are eligible first-time homebuyers by providing repayable down payment assistance loans of up to $37,500. This allows homebuyers to consider purchasing a home with as little as 2.5% for the down payment. This program is available until March 2020.

According to the BC Housing website, to be considered, you must:

- "Be a Canadian citizen or permanent resident for the last five years;
- Have lived in British Columbia for at least the full 12 months preceding your application;
- Be a first-time homebuyer who has not owned an interest in a principal residence anywhere in the world at any time and has never received a first-time homebuyer's exemption or refund;
- Purchase a home that is $750,000 or less;
- Be eligible for a high-ratio, insured first mortgage for the home.

- The combined, gross household income of all individuals on the title must not exceed $150,000; and
- The home being purchased must be used as the principal residence of all individuals on the title for five years after purchasing."

For more information, *Google: BC HOME Partnership*.

BUSINESS-FOR-SELF STATED INCOME PROGRAM

This program is designed for self-employed borrowers who are unable to provide traditional income verification but have a proven two-year history of managing their credit and finances responsibly.

Eligible borrowers have typically owned a small business for a minimum of two years, which can be confirmed through third-party, arm's length documents (a tax return completed by an accountant, business license and/or GST number). The borrower can then "state" their annual income, within reason, based on the industry standards, to qualify for the mortgage amount. Each mortgage insurer has its own guidelines to which borrowers must conform.

For more information:

Google: CMHC Self-Employed

Google: Genworth Business For Self (Alt. A) Program

Google: Canada Guaranty Low Doc Advantage™

DOWN PAYMENT: NON-TRADITIONAL/ BORROWED/FLEX DOWN

This option allows a borrower to purchase without having to save the full 5% down payment. A monthly payment, based on the borrowed funds used, will be added to the borrower's liabilities. Higher default mortgage premiums will apply.

For more information:

Google: CHMC Non-Traditional Sources of Down Payment

Google: Genworth Borrowed Down Payment Program

Google: Canada Guaranty Flex 95 Advantage™

ENERGY EFFICIENT REBATE AND INCENTIVE PROGRAMS

These are programs dedicated to energy efficiency and conservation for residential and commercial future energy needs, which currently include innovative clean energy (ICE) fund programs and utility energy efficiency programs. In BC, programs are currently offered for oil and heat pump incentives, BC Hydro PowerSmart options and FortisBC PowerSense rebate programs.

188

For more information:
Google: BC Gov energy efficiency conservation programs.

GREEN HOME/ENERGY EFFICIENCY PROGRAMS

Through these programs, homebuyers purchasing an energy-efficient home or making energy-saving renovations can be eligible for a refund of up to 25% on their mortgage default insurance premium.

For more information:
Google: CMHC Green Home
Google: Genworth Energy-Efficient Housing Program
Google: Canada Guaranty Energy-Efficient Advantage Program

MCAP 79

This innovative new product, launched in March 2017, offers the conventional borrower (with a down payment of 21% or more) a lower interest rate option, up to 0.5% off MCAP's standard rates, with a 1% upfront fee. It's a way for borrowers to have lower payments and potentially greater savings over the full term of their mortgage. To learn more, contact your mortgage broker.

NEW TO CANADA

Through these programs, qualified homebuyers who have immigrated or relocated to Canada within the last five years are eligible to purchase a property with as little as a 5% down payment.

For more information:

Google: CMHC Newcomer

Google: Genworth New To Canada

Google: Canada Guaranty Maple Leaf Advantage™

PURCHASE PLUS IMPROVEMENTS

This option is designed for qualified homebuyers who want to make improvements to their newly purchased property immediately after taking possession. Down payment requirements are based on the "as-improved" value of the property. For high-ratio purchases, the improvements usually cannot exceed 10% of the "as-improved" property value, or $40,000. Some lenders will consider this program for conventional purchases, where the improvement limits can be as high as $60,000. For the high-ratio files, each mortgage insurer has its own program requirements.

For more information:

Google: CMHC Improvement

Google: Genworth Purchase Plus Improvements Program

Google: Canada Guaranty Purchase Advantage Plus™

SECOND HOME/VACATION HOME/FAMILY PLAN

Some borrowers look to these programs to help them add a second home to their portfolio. It could be a second property in the city to reduce the weekly commute, a cottage at the lake for weekend getaways or a place for your child to live while going to school. There are mortgage programs offered by two of the three mortgage insurers that allow Canadians to be able to purchase a second home with as little as a 5% down payment.

For more information:

Google: Genworth Vacation/Secondary Homes Program

Google: Canada Guaranty Lifestyle Advantage™

PROPERTY TRANSFER TAX EXEMPTIONS

In BC, buyers are charged property transfer tax (PTT) when completing purchases or making changes in ownership to a property's title. The tax is charged at a rate of 1% on the first $200,000, 2% on the portion of the fair market value greater than $200,000 and up to and including $2,000,000, and 3% on the portion of the fair market value greater than $2,000,000.

First-time homebuyers may be exempt from paying the PTT for principal residences up to $500,000, which can translate into savings of up to $8,000. Partial exemptions are given between $500,000 and up to $525,000. For this exemption, the buyer must not have previously owned property anywhere in the world. Other provinces may also have their own first-time homebuyer rebate programs to source.

For more information:
Google: PTT exemption first time homebuyer

Newly built homes or **newly subdivided units** priced up to $750,000 may be exempt from paying the PTT, potentially saving buyers up to $13,000. Partial exemptions are available on newly built homes priced from $750,000 to $800,000. For this exemption, the buyer does not need to be a first-time homebuyer.

For more information:
Google: PTT exemption newly built

HOME BUYERS' PLAN (HBP)

This program allows borrowers to withdraw up to $25,000 in a calendar year from their registered retirement savings plans (RRSPs) to buy or build a qualifying home for themselves or a related person with a disability. The funds must be paid back to the RRSP over a period of 15 years. If at least 1/15th of the withdrawal is not repaid to the RRSP each year, starting the second year following purchase, the portion of the withdrawal due that is not repaid is taxed as income.

For more information:
Google: Home buyers plan

NEW HOUSING GST REBATE BC

New homebuyers can apply for a rebate of the 5% GST if the purchase price is $350,000 or less. The rebate is equal to 36% of the GST to a maximum rebate of $6,300. There is also a proportional GST rebate for new homes costing between $350,000 and $450,000, but no rebate for homes priced at $450,000 and above.

For more information:

Google: GST/HST new housing rebate BC

For more cost-saving programs the Real Estate Board of Greater Vancouver (REBGV) also provides a great list. *Google: REBGV cost saving programs*.

CHAPTER 11
I Need Insurance?

t's baffling: mortgage loan insurance, mortgage life insurance, life insurance, title insurance, home insurance!?

This chapter will clarify each type of insurance offered. It will also help you determine what is needed to complete your mortgage and what options you have to ensure you, your family and your property are protected.

MORTGAGE LOAN INSURANCE

Just when we thought if was complicated enough with all the different types of insurances, here comes another. Mortgage loan insurance is also commonly known as mortgage default insurance or just mortgage insurance.

Mortgage insurance makes it possible for Canadians to buy homes sooner, with a lower down payment, while protecting lenders and helping to keep our housing sector healthy. As we've covered earlier, in Canada, mortgage loan insurance is required when homebuyers make a down payment of less than 20% of the purchase price.

194 To reduce risk, some lenders may require conventional mortgage borrowers to be insured, charging the insurance premium to the client. This lowers the lender's overall risk, while usually giving the borrower a better interest rate.

Mortgage loan insurance is available from the Canada Mortgage and Housing Corporation (CMHC, a Crown corporation) and from private mortgage loan insurers, Genworth and Canada Guaranty.

All mortgage loan insurance sold in Canada is guaranteed by the federal government. If a borrower defaults on a loan, the government will cover any losses to the lender. Loans protected by CMHC insurance are 100% guaranteed, and those protected by private insurers Genworth and Canada Guaranty are 90% guaranteed. This means that lenders face no or low default risk on guaranteed mortgages, but borrowers must qualify under the insurer's guidelines. Government regulations on these guidelines have been tightened continuously since 2012.

CMHC

CMHC was launched in 1954 and is considered Canada's authority on housing, contributing to the stability of the housing market and financial system.

The organization provides support to Canadians in housing need and offer objective housing research and tools. I have provided CMHC's premium chart, but I recommend you also check out *cmhc-schl.gc.ca*. It is an extensive online resource offering information on buying a home, mortgage loan insurance, renting, green housing, aging in place and programs. The programs extend deeper into CMHC's initiatives and management of affordable housing, research and stats, mortgage-backed securities, Canadian mortgage bonds and Canadian registered covered bonds.

There is an endless amount of information provided by CMHC on the Canadian housing market. If you are so inclined, you can get regular updates on the Canadian housing conditions and trends by signing up for CMHC's Housing Observer Online, *cmhc.ca/observer/*. You can also do your own research on Canada's housing markets through CMHC's Housing Market Information Portal by *googling: CMHC HMI portal*. It's a very robust program offering detailed national stats on new housing, rentals, household population, core housing need and more.

195

In a couple of chapters of this book, I've referred to CMHC's free online *Home Buying Step by Step* guide and workbook. The workbook includes a five-step process with easy-to-fill-in sections from home budgets, financing needs, home comparison charts, a change of address checklist and a guide on when to perform maintenance on your property. Visit *cmhc.ca/stepbystep*.

CMHC also has an award-winning free app, the CMHC Mobile KIT, which includes mortgage calculators such as the mortgage affordability calculator. They are no match for getting the real thing with a mortgage broker, but they do provide good estimates.

By *googling: CMHC premiums*, you can use the chart (as seen on the next page) to estimate your expected insurance premiums manually, or you can access the CMHC premium calculator and other excellent calculators, such as the household budget calculator, by *googling: CMHC home-buying tools*.

CMHC MORTGAGE LOAN INSURNCE PREMIUMS

LOAN-TO-VALUE	PREMIUM ON TOTAL LOAN	PREMIUM ON INCREASE TO LOAN AMOUNT FOR PORTABILITY
Up to and including 65%	0.60%	0.60%
Up to and including 75%	1.70%	5.90%
Up to and including 80%	2.40%	6.05%
Up to and including 85%	2.80%	6.20%
Up to and including 90%	3.10%	6.25%
Up to and including 95%	4.00%	6.30%
90.01% to 95% — Non-Traditional Down Payment**	4.50%	6.60%

Premiums in Manitoba, Ontario and Quebec are subject to provincial sales tax. The provincial sales tax cannot be added to the loan amount.

** Down Payment Requirements — Traditional sources of down payment include: Applicant's savings, RRSP withdrawal, funds borrowed against proven assets, sweat equity (<50% of min. required equity), land unencumbered, proceeds from sale of another property, non-repayable gift from immediate relative, equity grant (non-repayable grant from federal, provincial or municipal agency). Non-traditional sources of down payment include: Any source that is arm's length to and not tied to the purchase or sale of the property, such as borrowed funds, gifts and 100% sweat equity.

CREDIT | Canada Mortgage and Housing Corporation *https://www.cmhc-schl.gc.ca/en/co/moloin/moloin_005.cfm* as of January 2018

Genworth

Canada's largest private residential mortgage insurer providing mortgage default insurance for Canadian residential mortgages for over two decades. *Homeownership.ca* is a resource Genworth provides, offering excellent information on the process of buying a home.

I have included Genworth's standard premium chart. They also have additional specialty program premium charts available on their website. (*Google Genworth premiums.*) They offer many calculators to help calculate mortgage insurance costs, affordability and payments. (*Google Genworth calculator.*)

GENWORTH CANADA PREMIUM RATE TABLE

STANDARD PREMIUM RATE CHART			INCLUDES THE FOLLOWING PRODUCTS*
LTV Ratio	Premium Rate	Top-Up Premium	• Homebuyer 95 Program
Up to 65%	0.60%	0.60%	• Borrowed Down Payment Program*
65.01% - 75%	1.70%	5.90%	• Family Plan Program
75.01% - 80%	2.40%	6.05%	• Progress Advance Program
80.01% - 85%	2.80%	6.20%	• New to Canada Program
85.01% - 90%	3.10%	6.25%	• Purchase Plus Improvements Program
90.01% - 95%	4.00%	6.30%	• Vacation/Secondary Home Program (Type A)

*For Borrowed Down Payment Program (LTV 90.01-95%) the standard premium rate is 4.50% and the premium for portability/top-up is 6.60%

CREDIT | Genworth Canada *http://genworth.ca/en/lenders/premium-rate-table.aspx* as of January 2018

Canada Guaranty

In 2010, a Canadian private investor group comprising the Ontario Teachers' Pension Plan and National Mortgage Guaranty Holdings Inc. acquired AIG United Guaranty Mortgage Insurance Company Canada. This transaction created the only 100% Canadian-owned private mortgage insurance company, the Canada Guaranty Mortgage Insurance Company (Canada Guaranty). Canada Guaranty provides unique default insurance options to help Canadians own sooner. Their premium chart is available on the next page, and they too have an online resource where you can learn more about their products and services at *canada-guaranty.ca/homebuyers#* or through their app, Canada Guaranty.

CANADA GUARANTY PREMIUM RATES AT A GLANCE

LOAN-TO-VALUE RATIO	STANDARD PREMIUM RATES		LOW DOC ADVANTAGE™		RENTAL ADVANTAGE™	
	Single	Port. Top-up	Single	Port. Top-up	Single	Port. Top-up
≤ 65%	0.60%	0.60%	1.50%	3.00%	1.45%	3.15%
65.01 - 75%	1.70%	5.90%	2.60%	6.50%	2.00%	3.45%
75.01 - 80%	2.40%	6.05%	3.30%	7.00%	2.90%	4.30%
80.01 - 85%	2.80%	6.20%	3.75%	7.50%		
85.01 - 90%	3.10%	6.25%	5.85%	9.00%		
90.01 - 95%	4.00%	6.30%				
Flex 95 Advantage™	4.50%	6.60%				

B.C. HOME PARTNERSHIP PROGRAM

LOAN-TO-VALUE RATIO	PREMIUM RATES
80.01% - 85%	2.80%
85.01% - 90%	4.00%
90.01% - 95%	4.50%
NOTE: Mortgage insurance premiums are non-refundable.	

CREDIT | Canada Guaranty *http://www.canadaguaranty.ca/products-at-a-glance/* as of January 2018

MORTGAGE LIFE INSURANCE

Mortgage life insurance is a form of insurance specifically designed to repay a mortgage. If the policyholder dies while the mortgage life insurance is in place, the policy pays out an amount sufficient to repay the outstanding mortgage.

Mortgage Protection Plan (MPP)

Through each mortgage brokerage, clients have access to a Mortgage Life Insurance Plan with their mortgage approval. A common policy offered is the Mortgage Protection Plan (MPP) by Manulife. The main benefit of this type of policy is that it is not attached to the lender, so it can be transferred to future properties if you move.

This is important, as the life insurance premiums you pay increase with age. If you had to break your mortgage contract and start with new insurance, your premiums could be significantly higher.

The Manulife Mortgage Protection Plan (MPP) helps make sure your dreams are protected in two ways:

199

Mortgage Life Insurance: This insurance is about helping you protect your investment. It's one thing, a very important thing, your family never has to worry about if you are not around to make the mortgage payments.
- Maximum coverage is $1 million.
- There is no waiting period for coverage.
- Life benefits are paid directly to the lender when a claim is completed.

Total Disability Insurance: Even a temporary disability can prevent you from working and making your mortgage payments. This is an insurance policy borrowers should review and consider carefully, especially those who are in the early years of their careers. This insurance is a good supplement to employment disability plans that only pay out 60% to 85% of your income.
- Maximum benefit is $10,000 per month
- Maximum benefit period is 24 months
- The qualification period is 60 days (that is, you must be disabled for more than 60 days for the benefit to kick in).

Other great features of the MPP include:
- Portable coverage. Once insured, if you move, refinance or increase your mortgage amount, the policy remains in force. MPP coverage can also be increased to cover any increase in debt.
- Immediate temporary protection. As soon as you sign and provide payment information, you are protected.
- A complementary insurance needs analysis is provided.
- 60-day money-back guarantee. You can review your coverage in detail, and if you change your mind within the first 60 days, you will receive a full refund of any premiums paid.
- You can cancel your insurance at any time. (Past the 60-day money-back guarantee there is no refund of premiums already paid.)

Lender's Mortgage Insurance

Each lender offers its own branded mortgage life insurance option. Some will note the cost of the insurance on the mortgage commitment while others, such as some banks and credit unions, will present these options to you at the branch signing. Terms, costs and maximum coverage vary between lenders. This insurance, unlike MPP, is not portable if the mortgage is transferred to a new lender.

200

LIFE INSURANCE

There are two main types of life insurance:

1. **Term Life Insurance**

    Provides insurance coverage for a limited period of time, such as 10 or 20 years. It is perhaps the easiest to understand and has the lowest initial cost.

2. **Permanent Life Insurance**

    Permanent insurance is more complex and tends to cost more than term, but it offers additional benefits. Whole life is the most well-known and simplest form of permanent life insurance. There are also other kinds of permanent life insurance.

If there are people who depend on you, life insurance is a protection policy to consider seriously. To learn about your options and see what product best aligns with your needs, it is best to set up an appointment with an insurance broker or financial planner. Most brokers have reputable financial planners and insurance brokers they can connect you to if needed.

PROPERTY AND FIRE INSURANCE

Property insurance provides financial reimbursement to the owner or renter of a building and its contents in the event of damage or theft. Different types of policies include homeowner's insurance, renter's insurance, flood insurance and earthquake insurance. Fire insurance covers damage or loss to a property because of fire. For condos, fire insurance is typically paid by the strata corporation from the strata fees. Policies are provided with the Annual General Meeting (AGM) minutes. Lenders usually require fire insurance confirmation prior to mortgage funding, which your solicitor provides to the lender. Most mortgage brokers will have connections to insurance brokers if you require contacts.

TITLE INSURANCE

With an increase in title fraud claims, more and more homeowners are protecting themselves with title insurance, and more lenders now require it as a condition of the mortgage. Title insurance not only protects what may happen in the future (title fraud), but it also has protection for things that may have happened before the purchase, such as pre-existing work orders or zoning violations. Usually the solicitor will arrange for the purchase of title insurance, both of which are at the borrower's cost.

There are two broad types of title insurance:

1. **Lender Policy**

   Protects the lender's interest in your mortgage and lasts as long as you have your mortgage. The price is based on the mortgage amount. This is the policy required by lenders as a condition of their mortgage.

2. **Homeowner Policy**

   Covers the homeowner, lasts as long as you or your heirs own the property (not the duration of the mortgage) and is priced based on the property value. Your solicitor can arrange this insurance on your behalf at the time of purchase, or the policy can be purchased at a later time.

The cost of title insurance varies and depends on the location, type and value of the transaction. It tends to average from $150 to $350, but may also be higher.

For an online quote, *google: First Canadian Title (FCT) Homeowner Policy or Stewart Title Calculator.*

CHAPTER 12

Preparing for the Extras, Before and After

Too many homebuyers are caught scrambling on their closing date because they aren't prepared for the common costs associated with buying a home. Below is a review of the closing costs that are often part of the mortgage process. Lenders may request you show proof of having 1.5% of the purchase price on hand in addition to the down payment to make sure you're capable of covering these costs.

Once you own a home, the costs of maintenance can also be shocking. Later, we look at how to budget so you won't be caught unprepared.

BEFORE

CLOSING COSTS

Appraisal Fees ($250 to $500+): If the property is insured by one of the three mortgage default insurers, the appraisal cost is covered by them. If they are not able to confirm the value through their automated valuation programs, they will arrange for an appraisal appointment.

For most conventional loans and refinances, a lender will require a complete appraisal at your cost. If the property has a rental component, a schedule A may also be requested to provide a rent projection on the unit based on market trends in the neighbourhood. This may be referred to as an economic rent assessment. If the property fits certain criteria, occasionally the lender's automated valuation program can be used instead of completing a full appraisal.

Home Inspection ($350 to $500+): A home inspection is not required by lenders. This cost is incurred if the buyers feel it necessary to complete an inspection.

Legal Fees and Disbursements ($750 to $1500+): Legal fees can vary from one solicitor to the next. Property complexities and instructions provided by the lenders (e.g., if there are any debts to be paid out) can add to the costs of the legal fees. Disbursements include costs such as couriers, photocopying, land title fees, law society fees and state of title certificates. Property taxes and strata costs will also be adjusted by the solicitor on the statement of adjustments.

> **Statement of Adjustments (SOA):** A statement of adjustments will be provided by your solicitor prior to or at your appointment. It will show the reconciliation for legal fees and disbursements as well as the property transfer tax, title insurance, mortgage proceeds, deposits paid and the adjustments between the seller's and buyer's portions of property taxes, strata fees, etc. Calculations are based on the **adjustment date** selected in the contract of purchase and sale. See sample on page 87.

LINGO!

ADJUSTMENT DATE

The date determined on the contract of purchase and sale that the solicitors will use to balance the costs of the property between the seller and the buyer. This will be reflected on the statement of adjustments provided by the solicitors.

205

IMPORTANT! If your mortgage is completed with a private lender, the borrower is responsible for **both** the borrower and lender's legal expenses.

Moving Costs: It's important to budget for moving costs. Some things to consider include:

- Moving van or storage rental;
- Hiring a moving company and cleaners;
- Renting bins, purchasing boxes or other packing supplies;
- Move-in and move-out fees for strata properties (usually accounted for by your solicitor on the SOA);
- Utilities, phone and internet transfer fees;
- Fire insurance costs; and
- Canada Post forwarding

Penalty Fees (Three-Months' Interest or IRD): If the mortgage is a refinance or you've sold property to buy this one and can't (or it doesn't make sense to) port the mortgage to your new property, you may also have to budget for prepayment penalties. Depending on the mortgage product and lender, the penalties will be either three-months' interest or the interest rate differential calculated by that lender, as discussed on page 102.

Property Transfer Tax (1% to 3%): In BC, buyers are charged property transfer tax when completing purchases or making changes in ownership to a property's title. The tax is charged at a rate of 1% on the first $200,000 of the fair market value, 2% on the portion greater than $200,000 and up to and including $2,000,000, and 3% on the portion of the fair market value greater than $2,000,000. There are exemptions for first-time homebuyers when the purchase price is below $500,000 and for all buyers purchasing new builds with values less than $750,000. For more information, *google BC PTT*. Other provinces have their own land transfer tax arrangements and costs. These vary greatly from province to province and the territories. Alberta and Saskatchewan are on the low end of the scale, having marginal land title transfer fees. BC and Ontario are at the highest end for transfer taxes, with the municipality of Toronto charging an additional land transfer tax to homebuyers.

206

Realtor Fees: Typically, the seller pays the realtor fees in a home sale transaction, which are then split in some capacity between the seller's agent and the buyer's agent. Unless there are prior arrangements made where the buyer is taking responsibility for the costs, or part of the costs, the seller will pay the realtor fees from the proceeds of the sale. Standard realtor fees are usually 7% on the first $100,000 and 2.5% on the remainder.

Title Insurance ($150+): Title insurance can protect the owners and lenders against losses incurred from numerous title risks as described on page 201. The lender policy fee can be deducted by the lender before the mortgage is advanced if they arrange the insurance; otherwise, it is usually included as part of the disbursements made by the solicitor. Borrowers will have to advise their solicitors if they wish to purchase the homeowner's policy.

AFTER

HOME MAINTENANCE AND BUDGET

CMHC's *Homebuying Step by Step* guide and workbook is a fantastic reference for this section.

Earlier, we discussed the importance of purchasing based on your budget. Now **207** that the purchase is complete and you can move from estimates to hard numbers, it is worthwhile to review and update your budget to factor in changes in home insurance, utility services, property taxes and strata fees, etc.

The workbook also provides a full maintenance calendar, with a guide to monthly upkeep. It also addresses major projects to focus on once a year and every two to five years. Your costs will vary based on the type of property and work needed.

The guide and workbook covering the budget, maintenance schedule and more can be found at *cmhc.ca/stepbystep*.

YOUR EMERGENCY FUND

As a homeowner, it is also a great idea to set aside some funds each month into an emergency fund to cover unexpected expenses, including the inevitable major repairs. The commonly recommended amount is 5% of your household income.

In addition to an emergency fund account, I also recommend having a "lifeline" account: a line of credit or home equity line of credit—with room to spare. Emergencies or major repairs can come at any time, and the price tag may be much higher than what is currently in your emergency fund. Hot water tanks, furnaces, and strata special levies can require immediate action and cash. Ensure that you always have access to funds should they be needed. Once you have a mortgage, you don't want to ever miss a payment.

CHAPTER 13
The Mortgage Broker Advantage

According to the Canadian Mortgage Housing Cooperation (CMHC) Mortgage Consumer surveys, the number of Canadians who arrange their mortgage through a broker continues to increase in all categories, including refinancing, repeat buyers, renewers and first-time buyers.

Among first-time buyers, 55% in 2016 and 2017 used mortgage brokers, a trend driven by a desire for expert advice and demand for the best rates and products.

This is a surprising stat when you think of the limited time mortgage brokers have been around. The national mortgage broker association, Mortgage Professionals Canada (MPC), was established in 1994. In BC, our provincial association, the Canadian Mortgage Brokers Association - British Columbia (CMBA-BC) was established in 1990.

Banks have been around a lot longer and have generational recognition, gaining loyalty through their obvious presence in communities. In 2017, in fact, as Canada celebrated its 150th year, so did CIBC. And as amazing as that is, CIBC is the youngster among the country's major banks. That same year RBC was 153, TD was 162, BMO was celebrating its 200th birthday, and Scotiabank dates back to 1671, a sprightly 346 years old.

210

Canadian banks are impressive on a global scale as well.

RBC has 80,000 staff serving 16 million people in 37 countries. It is Canada's largest bank, and one of the largest banks in the world based on market capitalization. It had $1.2 trillion in assets as of 2017.

TD serves 25 million people and has 80,000 employees, with $1.3 trillion in assets as of April 30, 2017.

Scotiabank serves 23 million people and has 88,000 employees, with assets of $896 billion as of October 31, 2016.

BMO serves 12 million people, has more than 45,000 employees and had total assets of $719 billion as of April 30, 2017.

CIBC has total assets of $501.4 billion, 11 million clients and 44,000+ employees.

Canada is a small fish swimming in a big ocean, but our financial system has achieved impressive global growth and our banks are known as some of the most secure in the world.

What does this have to do with your future mortgage?

Well, there is no question we need banks. Strong Canadian banks strengthen our economy as well as Canada's global position and presence.

However, being the biggest and oldest doesn't mean you are the best at everything. Being large can help organizations compete in the marketplace, but smaller companies with specializations or niche products also have unique competitive advantages.

The broker market has continued to grow substantially since its inception because of resourcefulness, adaptability and customer support. Our product recommendations are not driven by a push to meet sales quotas. As independent agents, brokers can truly work in your best interest, as there are no direct ties between our pay cheques and any company's shareholder demands.

We are paid by lenders and have a wide selection of lenders to choose from including banks, monoline lenders, credit unions, B lenders and private lenders and investors. Furthermore, unlike mortgage specialists working at a bank, mortgage brokers are required to be licensed sub-mortgage broker, completing a provincially regulated course, such as the **UBC Sauder School of Business Mortgage Brokerage in British Columbia course**.

Brokers have access to hundreds of mortgage products from a variety of lenders, each with their own specialty in the marketplace. What one lender may not be willing to do, another may have it as its niche. Different lender policies and guidelines create a unique opportunity for mortgage brokers to tailor products to individual buyers. The broker channel is like being able to order a specialty drink from Starbucks (grande, decaf, soy, extra-hot, half-sweet caramel macchiato to stay, please), as opposed to being limited to the drip brew from your financial institution (coffee?).

Knowing your needs, your broker's objective is to work the mortgage market to find a solution that fits. The goal is always the same: minimize the overall borrowing costs, provide a damn good solution and monitor it.

LINGO!

UBC SAUDER SCHOOL OF BUSINESS, MORTGAGE BROKERAGE IN BRITISH COLUMBIA COURSE

According to the school's website, the Mortgage Brokerage in British Columbia course is the only course specifically designed to satisfy the minimum educational requirements to become registered with the Financial Institutions Commission (FICOM) Registrar of Mortgage Brokers as a sub-mortgage broker in British Columbia.

CHAPTER 14
Moving with the Changes

Our move back to Richmond served us well. Jack appreciated our home as much as we did—the neighbours, daycare, community and activities available were great. The waterpark, trampoline park, arena and theatre, all within walking distance, were extra bonuses when he was finally old enough to enjoy them.

The cherry on top happened about a year after our move. A desirable position opened up at Mark's previous golf club. It was his dream job, with a membership and club he cares for and highly respects. And it was only seven minutes from home (again).

We lived our comfortable lives for the longest stretch in one place since we had reconnected, a total of four years.

But now we were expecting baby number two, which ultimately meant some more changes.

My first brokerage was TMG The Mortgage Group, an amazing company with a long history in the industry. I connected with many incredible colleagues, and I was fortunate to be mentored by smart, talented and caring brokers. They love what they do and are so good at it.

Having spent many years there, I felt it was time to make some adjustments to better position myself for the growth of our family alongside the growth of my business. Xeva Mortgage was a brokerage with three powerhouse women in the top 75 brokers in Canada, women who achieved repeat success while raising families. Not only were these women successful, but they were willing to teach, share and mentor—and I wanted to learn more.

I moved to Xeva at the same time I made a second pivotal move, shifting our home search into high gear. I had been looking casually since 2012 and even had an "open house" series on my blog that I eventually began to use to check out homes of interest for our family.

I was finding that prices were rapidly moving out of our range in the areas of interest to us, or we were not willing to spend the money asked once we factored in the limited amenities and long commutes.

It was now 2015, and the market for townhouses in desirable areas and single-family dwellings was HOT, HOT, HOT. Subject-free offers were commonplace, and mortgage brokers and lenders alike were having to change strategies and adapt to help clients through the resulting unpredictability.

I had been experiencing the no-subject situation with my clients on repeat for months. Now we had to jump into that rat race ourselves. With the new baby on it's way, it was a crucial time for us to move, so we either had to lower our expectations on the property or expand our search area again.

We had our condo up for sale, but condos were not hot, at least not in our area. They were down, in some cases way down. Lots of new builds were underway in Richmond, so we were up against steep competition.

We decided that to maximize our mortgage and get into a home we wanted, we would sell the property on Oxford too. It was a sad moment for me. We spoke to our tenant to ask if she was interested in buying.

Time felt tight. Between summer coming to an end, Mark's work schedule, me changing companies, Jack starting kindergarten, and the baby coming, I wasn't sure how we were going to get it done in time.

In a moment of timing bliss, we had an offer on our Richmond condo, albeit not a great offer, and an offer on Oxford by our tenant. In both cases, the offers were far lower than I had ever imagined we would accept. We were going to lose on Riverport, and after nine years, the small gain on Oxford felt like a loss.

However, most of the down payment for our new home would come from the equity we had built up by making our mortgage payments on Riverport. The Oxford property had supported us through two previous purchases and the launch and growth of my business. More than a home, it was a lifeline.

In the new home search, Vancouver was never an option, even in 2012. Richmond and Burnaby were out as of 2013, New Westminster and Ladner, with few exceptions, were out as of 2014, Tsawassen and White Rock were out as of 2014 as well, and South Surrey was too far away.

In 2014, our realtor introduced us to Sunshine Hills in North Delta. We really liked it. However, like everywhere else I had already scouted, prices were starting to jump. We decided to expand the search but stay in North Delta, stretching north and in some cases south from Sunshine Hills.

Once it looked like the condos were going to sell, I reviewed our calendar and realized that Mark and I only had one day together in the coming month to look at homes. We asked our realtor to book all possible viewings and when the day came, toured home after home, back to back. I lost count, but we saw somewhere around 10 properties.

At the end of the day Mark and I each made a short list of our favourites. Both of our top two picks were the two properties we hadn't been able to view yet. (Goes to show the limited options available!) Both were in our preferred communities, one north and one south of Sunshine Hills and both within a stone's throw of an elementary school.

The first of the two, an adorable Cape Cod-style home, turned out to need a lot of work. That left one. Jack and I went on our own, no realtor and no Mark. Jack liked this house because there was Tim Hortons Timbits. It won my heart because it checked off more boxes on our dream list than I'd ever imagined.

216

There were so many people at the open house, and they were calling more people to come see it. As Jack ate more donuts, I walked around adding up the checkmarks on the virtual list in my head.

We left, and I called our realtor first. Then I called Mark to let him know we had to make an offer, and it would probably have to be subject free. We learned there were multiple offers, so we had to place our offer by six p.m. the next night, meaning that—once again—we'd be putting an offer on a property Mark hadn't seen. This time, though, the risks were greater. Our rental property sale hadn't finalized, financing had not been verified and our decision on the price we would offer came down to the final minutes before the deadline. Our best foot forward.

I didn't think we were going to get it. It was hard to sit still, concentrate or even think.

We needed to confirm the Oxford sale, we needed to finalize financing, and I was crossing my fingers Mark was going to like the home. Sometime after nine p.m., a couple of hours after we got confirmation of the subject removal on the Oxford property, we got the call: it was ours.

Off I went, a Saturday morning last-minute stop to my bank before heading out of town for the August long weekend, scrambling to pool all our available funds for the deposit.

Then it was the long wait to move in, which was good. Packing while pregnant should be a long, slow process. The closing was the first week of October, two weeks before the baby was due.

Reflecting on the Holmes and Rahe Stress Scale, fall 2015 was probably our most stressful time as a family. A recent business change for me, the move, the arrival of our daughter, Jack's fifth birthday (five is a special age, especially when there is a new baby to demand Mom's and Dad's attention). Mark was promoted and started his new position, and very sadly, his grandfather passed away. All this happened over a few short weeks, crossing over Thanksgiving and Halloween. Just when we felt we made it over that mountain, we realized Christmas was right around the corner.

It was all-consuming and overwhelming. It has probably taken me two years to decompress from that time in my life.

Happy moments, sad moments, holy-shit moments, and moments I don't care to remember. It was life being life, at its prime.

Regardless of the whirlwind start to our new home, though, we all loved it. We settled in perfectly.

Here is a secret your realtor wishes you knew but won't tell you: your "must have" list will change as you begin to understand the trade-offs between location, affordability, square footage and features. And that's okay. Some of your must-haves will drift into the like-to-have column. But writing down the details of your dreams makes it much more likely you'll spot the opportunities before they fly by.

First, write down 10 characteristics of the new home you'd like to see yourself in.

Now, rank them in order of importance:

1.

2.

3.

4.

5.

6.

7.

8.

9.

10.

Notes:

CHAPTER 15
Trending in the Real Estate Market

The Canadian Real Estate Association (CREA) states that a national sales-to new listings ratio between 40% and 60% is consistent with a balanced national housing market. Volumes below and above this range indicate buyers' and sellers' markets, respectively.

A BUYERS' MARKET

When there are more homes for sale than there are buyers, it can result in slower price increases, and it puts more power and options in the hands of buyers versus sellers. Multiple offer situations tend to disappear along with no-subject offers. At the same time, it can mean less inventory on the market as homeowners are less inspired to sell.

A SELLERS' MARKET

When there are more buyers then there are homes available, we have what is considered a sellers' market. A rise in price above the long-term average rate of inflation is usually the result, along with crazy open houses, bidding wars with multiple and no-subject offers and a general shift of power to sellers. ("No, we're definitely not leaving the drapes, and that roof is your problem!)

222

A BALANCED MARKET

When supply and demand are about the same, home prices typically rise in line with the long-term average rate of inflation.

MARKET CONDITIONS FOR DETACHED HOMES IN THE VANCOUVER AND ABBOTSFORD CENSUS METROPOLITAN AREA (CMA)

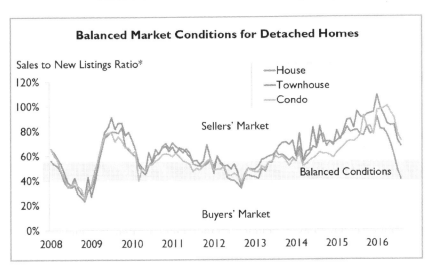

CREDIT | CMHC Housing Market Outlook for Vancouver and Abbotsford CMAs, 2016. Source: REBGV, CMHC calculations. *Seasonally adjusted

This graph from the CMHC Housing Market Outlook for Vancouver and Abbotsford CMAs, released in the fall of 2016, shows that it has mostly been a sellers' market for all types of property in the Greater Vancouver and Abbotsford region since 2014. The exception to that overall trend is the dip in late 2016 for houses, likely due to the regulatory changes that affected foreign buyers (implemented in August 2016) and high-ratio buyers (in October 2016).

This sellers' market has driven three strong trends in the lower mainland since 2014: low teaser list prices, well-over asking offers and subject-free offers. These are all common in sellers' markets.

LOW TEASER LISTING PRICE

In a sellers' market, it can be advantageous to list a property below its actual value to build interest in the aim of generating multiple offers. It doesn't always work, but when it does, it can lead to big returns for the seller. When making an offer, the list price is therefore not necessarily an exact representation of value, but a marketing tool for the selling agent. In this case, the hope to is to increase the volume of bids with the expectation of higher offers and few to no subjects.

OVER ASKING OFFERS

Both Vancouver and Toronto have been experiencing incredibly high over-asking offers in the last few years. Whether the property is listed with a low teaser list price or in line with current market prices, it has not been uncommon to see properties selling for $20,000 to $100,000+ over the asking price. Toronto's market has softened since its peak in the spring of 2017; unprecedented sale prices continue in Vancouver's downtown condo market.

SUBJECT-FREE OFFERS (NO-SUBJECT OFFERS)

Buyers in a bidding war may consider a no-subject offer: making an offer to purchase with no subjects. In a balanced market, prudently, offers usually include conditions that make the offer valid only when certain conditions are met: subject to buyer financing, a satisfactory inspection and review of property documents, for example. A subject-free offer is more attractive to the seller, as there is no delay for conditions to be removed. If the seller agrees to the offer, the property is sold and the contract is binding.

I've seen more subject-free offers in the past couple years than I thought I would see in my entire career.

Making a Subject-free Offer

If you feel you need to consider a subject-free offer for your purchase, I urge you to eliminate as much risk as you can. There is no guarantee that financing will be approved, as lenders do not review a file until there is an accepted contract in place. However, there are steps you can take to mitigate the risk involved.

224   In a typical subject offer, lenders are approving the following documentation to give the mortgage approval needed to remove subjects:

- Income documents;
- Down payment documents; and
- Property documents

Your mortgage brokers can review the income and down payment documents to know what the lender is likely to approve. It's the property that remains questionable. By providing the MLS listing and property disclosure statement (and if the property is strata, the strata form B, depreciation report or engineers report), before you make an offer, your broker can flag any potential concerns. It doesn't provide any guarantees, but it does help minimize the risk involved in a no-subject offer.

An article in REW/NEWS, "What It Takes to Win a Bidding War," addresses the now not-so-uncommon tactics of low listing prices to attract more buyers—and more bids, which leads to over-asking and subject-free offers. Author Lindsie Tomlinson says,

> "When buying a home, people normally expect a little give-and-take between the buyer and the seller. But in a multiple-offer situation, you are not negotiating with the seller—you are courting them. Your offer needs to be the most attractive to beat out all the others.

> "So how do you put together that winning offer? There's more to it than just going in with the highest price. Your offer needs the fewest possible number of subjects—or to be more accurate, no subjects.

> "If that sounds risky, well, it certainly can be. A no-subject offer means doing your homework before you offer, rather than after."

The article outlines what "doing your homework before, rather than after" means. This includes:

- **Home Inspection**

  A home inspection (a cost that you will not get back if your bid is not selected).

- **Documentation**

  If strata property, obtain all the documentation on the property and read it all. This includes, but not limited to:
  - Past two years of strata and AGM meeting minutes
  - Bylaws
  - Financial statements
  - Form B
  - Depreciation report (if available)
  - Engineer's report (if available)
  - Registered strata plan
  - Title search

- **Property Disclosure Statement**

  Obtain a copy and forward to your mortgage broker.

- **Oil scan**

  If the property is a house, check for oil tanks.

- **Financing**

  Get it in order. It's not worth being in breach of your contract if you are not able to get the mortgage you need for the purchase. However, understand that having everything in order does not mean an official approval is guaranteed.

- **Recent Sales**

  Have your realtor provide a list of recent sales in the neighbourhood for similar properties to determine market value.

- **Offer your best price.**

  Tomlinson states:

  "How much is this property worth to you? What's the price you'll be happy to pay for it? And at what price are you okay with letting someone else win it? Think about how you'll feel if someone else gets it for less than what you're willing to pay.

  "In a bidding war, you need to put your best foot forward and offer your highest price. You may not get a second chance. Sometimes a few offers are close and you get a chance to submit another one, but you should assume this won't happen."

- **Dates**

  Give completion and possession dates that best suit the seller.

- **Deposit**

  Include a copy of the deposit cheque with the offer. This demonstrates your seriousness and interest in the property.

When making an offer, it comes down to your team. With the right mortgage broker and realtor, your team will be working ahead of the curve to create strategies that make it possible for you to achieve your objectives.

Know the Risks of a Subject-Free Offer

The risks associated with making a subject-free offer can include:

1. The property may not be approved by lenders due to building issues such as extensive water damage, building repairs in progress, legal proceedings, the type of zoning or an inability to get insurer approval.
2. If the appraised economic life of the property isn't long enough for the required amortization, you may not be able to get financing. A property's economic life should be at least five years greater than the loan amortization.
3. If the offer price is higher than the appraised value, you will need to have the cash available for the shortfall—a lender will never loan more than the appraised value minus your down payment.

Example:

Say you make a no-subject offer of $750,000 expecting to put 20% ($150,000) for a down payment. The offer is accepted. An appraisal is completed per the lender's requirement, and the appraised value comes in at $725,000, $25,000 lower than the agreed purchase price. The lender will only lend based on the appraised value of $725,000 and not the purchase price of $750,000.

You must either:

- Put the 20% down on the appraised value, $145,000, plus $25,000 for the shortfall, for a down payment of $170,000; or
- Keep the investment of $150,000 the same, but $25,000 would now go to cover the shortfall and $125,000 for the down payment. This file would now be high ratio and not conventional, limiting the maximum amortization to 25 years. Insurance premiums would be applicable and included in the mortgage.

If you're not able to complete a purchase contract, the deposit will be lost to the seller. The seller also has the option to sue for further loss and damages, particularly if the property has decreased in value since the accepted offer.

THE CANADIAN MARKET RIGHT NOW

Nationally, the Canadian Real Estate Association (CREA) Housing Stats from September 2017 had all 13 markets with home prices up from a year ago—something that has not happened in nearly seven years with two-thirds of all local markets in balanced market territory. However, price trends continue to vary widely by region.

Looking at the national average pricing for December 2017, the numbers are extremely skewed by Canada's largest and most expensive markets, Greater Vancouver and Greater Toronto. The average would be $381,000 with these two markets removed, trimming $115,500 from the $496,500 national average.

CANADA HOME PRICE INDEX (HPI)
December 2017

MLS® HOME PRICE INDEX BENCHMARK PRICE

Composite HPI	December 2017	PERCENTAGE CHANGE VS.					
		1 month ago	3 months ago	6 months ago	12 months ago	3 years ago	5 years ago
Aggregate	$600,300	0.04	-0.17	2.63	9.11	34.60	48.32
Lower Mainland	$952,400	0.67	1.70	6.29	17.29	66.17	77.24
Greater Vancouver	$1,050,300	0.33	1.25	5.17	15.86	62.87	76.14
Fraser Valley	$765,900	1.34	2.67	8.82	20.91	75.20	80.98
Vancouver Island	$444,700	1.40	1.77	6.29	19.26	49.42	51.07
Victoria	$625,800	0.63	0.83	2.38	14.21	47.29	47.50
Calgary	$427,400	-0.76	-1.85	-1.94	-0.41	-5.89	11.51
Regina	$282,900	-0.42	-2.89	-5.00	-3.96	-2.20	-7.87
Saskatoon	$295,100	-0.54	-2.23	-3.74	-3.74	-7.01	-3.18
Guelph	$415,300	1.32	1.17	-1.53	13.06	37.79	53.63
Oakville-Milton	$683,400	-1.42	-3.55	-7.07	-0.76	35.50	58.07
Greater Toronto	$743,500	-0.16	-0.97	-8.29	7.19	42.54	63.07
Ottawa	$369,400	0.00	0.55	2.37	6.62	11.85	12.54
Greater Montreal	$330,900	0.12	1.00	2.15	5.42	10.89	13.46
Greater Moncton	$176,000	0.54	0.40	2.19	6.33	11.48	14.72

CREDIT | The Canadian Real Estate Association (CREA), *http://creastats.crea.ca/natl/*

PREDICTIONS

I have read many articles and economists' predictions about what is expected to happen, when the "bubble" will burst and where the hot and slow markets will be. In 2012, Alberta was leading house sales in Canada, and the Real Estate Investment Network (REIN) projected that Calgary would be the hottest investment city for the next three years. Then oil prices tanked. Buying during economic turmoil with declining prices can be a terrific investment, but it comes with an indefinite timeline.

Economic factors will always impact the real estate market. To be aware of what could happen is important, but you must still do what makes the most sense for you and your needs. There will always be cheerleaders for "Team Buy" and "Team Don't Buy." There will always be projections of price increases or bursting bubbles. There will always be the dynamics of rate changes, rule changes and lender guideline changes.

I cannot pretend to know what will happen. Economists, who spend all day, each day, researching the many variables at play, are still wrong far more than they are right. No one can truly predict what will happen next week, never mind what will happen a year or five years from now.

What I do know: I know that property values move steadily upwards over the long term. This has been the case since the dawn of the housing market.

Dustan Woodhouse, an expert mortgage broker in our industry, once wisely advised me that, "*The only economy that really matters is the one that sits between your very own two ears.*"

CHAPTER 16

Opportunity Awaits—Buy versus Rent

I n 2012, I wrote a blog contradicting a *Globe and Mail* article, "When Renting Is an Appetizing Option," by Dianne Maley. I'd been reading the same type of article for years.

I hold the same values and beliefs today as I did then, and I feel it is worthwhile to share my views again with you here:

> "*I am always amazed when I read these types of articles. More often than not, the couples interviewed are in very good financial positions and have a number of options when considering real estate purchases. Yet, every time, advisers advise them to wait and buy later. Save more money for four to five years and then consider buying once you have a LARGE savings fund built up, around 25%.*

232

"Why is this the only solution given? Especially when dealing with a volatile product such as real estate? Waiting four to five years could be good; however, considering the market we're in, buying in one to three years might be a better use of your money if prices drop and interest rates remain low. By sticking with a five-year buying plan, thousands of dollars in built-up equity could be missed. By not looking outside the three-bedroom house dream and considering a smaller unit, say a condo, potential ownership could be postponed for longer than hoped. What if prices don't go lower, interest rates go higher, and mortgage rules change again? I believe there is some "extra" value in entering the market with a lower-cost investment to start. Refinancing options can give you the opportunity to use your equity when you are ready to upgrade, while possibly keeping your first property as a rental.

"I urge couples and individuals to take a serious look at their financials. Understand that timing is important—but to take advantage of it, you also need to be watching the market. A plan that doesn't involve watching and understanding what's happening in the market and how interest rates are changing is a plan that could potentially cost you.

"Meet with a financial planner and a mortgage broker so you have experts working with your best interests in mind. Consider filling out a mortgage application, even if you feel you're not ready to buy now, to get an idea of what you can afford. Do it again in a year or 18 months. Review any changes and learn how they affect your buying power. By taking this simple step, you will be better able to identify when the time is right for you to purchase, taking into consideration your current income, down payment, expected mortgage approval and market prices."

On the other end of the spectrum, I recently read a *Globe and Mail* article by Duncan Hood published in September 2017, "Why Telling People to Rent Rather Than Buy Is Bad Advice." It spoke so clearly to my beliefs about ownership that I feel it's necessary to highlight the article here. Hood says, about his nerve-racking home purchase three years before:

"... In hindsight, buying my house was the right thing to do, but not because the market happened to catch fire after I did. It was the right thing to do because, after years of renting, I wanted a place of my own that I could pay off

before I retire. And besides, I could afford it. Now that I'm a homeowner, I realize that the value of your house is a pretty abstract number. If you're not planning to sell, and you can make your mortgage payments, it doesn't matter all that much where the market is going."

Hood wrote that if he had understood that idea sooner, he would have bought years before and been much closer to paying off his mortgage today. As a per- **233** sonal finance editor (with *MoneySense* magazine), he advised readers to rent and invest the difference. He continues:

That argument sounded convincing to me, but .... I now realize that real people, as opposed to soulless money robots, generally don't invest the difference; they spend it on Vitamixes and trips to Cancún. Even if they do sock away the money, most are terrible investors. According to a study by Dalbar, the average annual return in the real world over the past 20 years has been less than 3%.

He goes on to courageously (and humbly) admit that his financial situation is much better than it was three years ago because he ignored his own earlier advice.

Most Canadians dream of owning their home, which can then lead to bigger dreams and greater potential.

And most people around the world, including Canadians, buy property with a mortgage. Those who do have cash are usually financially savvy enough to know that being able to borrow at the low rates we have seen in recent years provides leverage to potentially make more money.

The fact that you can buy something of such substantial value and have a lender advance up to 95% of its value (97.5% if you are a first-time homebuyer in BC)—providing you can prove you have a steady income, decent credit and some funds of your own—it's crazy, really.

Why wouldn't you take advantage of this opportunity, considering the long-term returns of real estate?

In 2011 I wrote a blog entitled, "Is Buying in Metro Vancouver Worthwhile?" I included a graph similar to the one that follows, showing home prices from 1977 to 2011 with a clear upward trend on home values.

To the right is the Vancouver Residential Average Sale Prices graph, updated to include 1977 to 2017. As you can see, home prices fluctuate from one year to the next, up and down like scribbles on a chalkboard. But scale back and look at the big picture, the uniform "best-fit" diagonal line, and you see a sizable and steady growth pattern over the past 40 years.

VANCOUVER RESIDENTIAL AVERAGE SALE PRICES

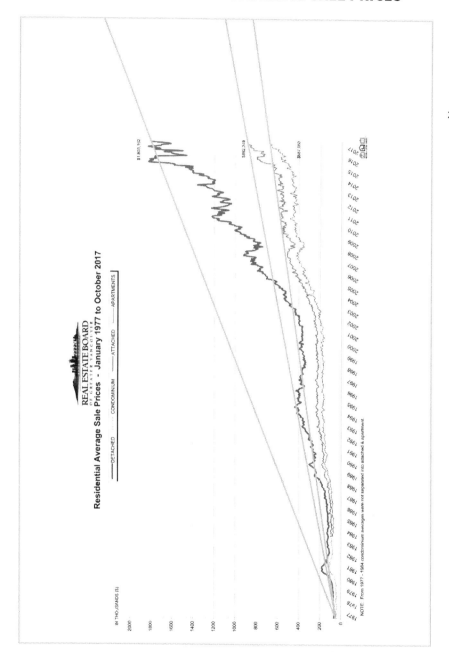

Looking at the Home Price Index (HPI) for Greater Vancouver in October 2017, prices have increased approximate 70% over the past six years. If you bought a home for $612,800 in October 2011, it was likely worth somewhere near $1,042,300 in October 2017. Where else are you able to access that kind of return with as little as 5% down, or $30,640?

HOME PRICE INDEX FOR GREATER VANCOUVER, OCT 2011

BENCH MARK	PRICE INDEX	1 MONTH +/-	6 MONTH +/-	1 YEAR +/-	3 YEAR +/-	5 YEAR +/-
RESIDENTIAL - ALL TYPES						
$612,800	160.2	-0.4	1.6	8.0	14.8	24.9
DETACHED						
$945,800	173.8	0.1	3.7	14.8	26.8	38.2
TOWNHOUSE						
$477,600	154.1	-0.4	0.7	5.0	10.6	21.4
APARTMENT						
$372,200	149.6	-0.8	-0.7	2.1	5.5	13.9

CREDIT | Real Estate Board of Greater Vancouver http://www.rebgv.org/home-price-index?region=Greater+Vancouver&type=all&date=2011-10-01

HOME PRICE INDEX FOR GREATER VANCOUVER, OCT 2017

BENCH MARK	PRICE INDEX	1 MONTH +/-	6 MONTH +/-	1 YEAR +/-	3 YEAR +/-	5 YEAR +/-
RESIDENTIAL - ALL TYPES						
$1,042,300	272.5	0.5	9.1	12.4	62.1	71.7
DETACHED						
$1,609,600	295.8	-0.5	5.4	4.0	61.0	72.4
TOWNHOUSE						
$802,400	258.9	2.0	10.5	17.7	62.7	71.0
APARTMENT						
$624,000	258.0	1.0	13.3	22.7	65.8	73.2

237

CREDIT | Real Estate Board of Greater Vancouver *http://www.rebgv.org/home-price-index?region=Greater+Vancouver&type=all&date=2017-10-01*

Let's take this a step further.

On that same purchase of $612,800 in 2011, let's assume a mortgage of 95% of the value. Mortgage loan insurance premiums at the time were 2.75%, with an interest rate of 3.5% (a competitive rate for 2011, but higher than the average interest rate over the past six years), amortized over 25 years.

$612,800 purchase price
− $30,640 down payment
$582,160 mortgage
+ $16,009 mortgage insurance
= **$598,169 total mortgage**

Over this six-year period, the homeowner would have paid approximately $114,800 in interest and $100,300 towards principal.

With a current market value of $1,042,300 and a remaining mortgage of approximately $498,000, the owner would have $544,300 in equity.

From the original $30,640 down payment invested, $16,009 insurance premiums paid and the $215,100 in principal and interest payments, a total of $261,749 invested, the six-year return on investment (ROI) would be nearly 108%, with an annualized ROI of over 11%.

$$ROI = \frac{(\$544,300 - \$261,749)}{\$261,749} = \textbf{108\%}$$

Today, the owners could refinance their home up to 80% of the value, accessing up to $335,840 of their equity. They could invest it in more property, stocks, RRSPs (for tax deductions) or other retirement plans to grow their nest egg, while their initial investment continues to increase in value and equity grows with future mortgage payments.

There is so much opportunity in real estate. It's my hope you consider rising to the occasion to invest—and continue to invest.

CHAPTER 17

The Rise

Within a year of our house purchase, the market had increased so drastically that we were able to refinance our home to consolidate some of the purchases we had made for the new, larger space, as well as to set us up for a major backyard landscaping project. Eighteen months after our purchase and six months after our refinance, with the extensive backyard project about to start, I put an offer on a second home. (The third property of the four we've bought together that Mark didn't see before the offer.)

I went against the grain—the market was hot, and both my husband and our realtor pointed out the timing was therefore bad. For me, however, this was a long-term investment, and this property will not be the last. Any chance I get, I want to invest, which drives my conservative husband crazy.

I believe that real estate is an incredible investment. Most of the properties I viewed at open houses over the years would have made money, and lots, had we just been able or willing at the time. Most have more than doubled in value in less than five years. That's not normal; however, good returns can still be expected over the long term.

242   There will also be dips in the market. Do I want you to sell in the dips? Not necessarily, but if I'm able to sell and upgrade for a small loss, then it might not be a bad move. The new property may eventually be valued at far more than the one I originally owned.

If you spend a bit of time and get the right real estate team and mortgage product—and you feel okay with some risk—you can do well. In some cases, very well.

There is always a chance you can lose on real estate, too. We did, with our Riverport property; we came close with Oxford as well. Yet the principal and interest payments our tenants and we made put us within reach of the impossible dream, a lovely detached family home in Vancouver's lower mainland, where we regained those losses and much more. Along the way, our homes were a forced savings plan for us that allowed us to stretch with the growing needs of our family.

It's been an exciting adventure and one that will continue. We have plans to eventually build a new home on our current lot, which has a view I love to wake up to each morning.

I hope I have inspired you to commit to making homeownership part of your future, so that you too can own your piece of this earth.

What role would you like real estate to play in your life over the next 10, 20 or 30 years? If you'd like real estate to serve as a wealth-building tool for you and your family, this is a good time to think about what that might look like and who you need on your team to achieve that.

Note your goals below—and go after them! Feel free to contact me if you want to discuss how we can get you there together.

GLOSSARY

All the Mortgage Lingo You Need
for Your Financing Toolkit

E ven though you may have heard these words before, or seen them throughout this book, I recommend reviewing them again to get a clear picture on how they may influence your mortgage approval. You can always refer to this list if needed, or ask your broker for clarification at any time.

For some of these terms, I have included my personal notes on things you may want to consider as you make your mortgage decision.

A LENDERS

Bank, credit union and monoline lenders, offering their best rates and products to A-type clients with good credit, qualified income and resources for down payment.

ADJUSTABLE-RATE MORTGAGE (ARM)

See Variable-Rate Mortgage

ADJUSTMENT DATE

The date determined on the contract of purchase and sale that the solicitors will use to balance the costs of the property between the seller and the buyer. This will be reflected on the statement of adjustments provided by the solicitors.

AMORTIZATION

Your mortgage *term* is the length of time your agreement with the lender covers, most commonly five years. The *amortization*, on the other hand, is the length of time it would take you to completely pay off your mortgage at the current rate of interest and payment schedule.

High-ratio borrowers (those whose down payment is less than 20% of the value of the home) are limited to 25-year amortizations.

For conventional mortgages (those with down payments are 20% or more of the value of the home), amortizations of 25 years or less can give borrowers better pricing; however, if lower payments are desired, 30-year and, in rare situations, 35-year amortizations may be requested.

In most cases, I recommend choosing the longest amortization available. The longer the amortization, the lower the payments. This is an important option for borrowers to maintain, should unexpected life changes arise. Job loss, illness and surprising housing costs like the unexpected need for a new furnace can put pressure on your monthly budget.

While your mortgage agreement will almost always allow you to make higher payments, the option to revert to the lower required payments—or to extend your amortization back to the original length—can provide welcome options during tough times.

If you want to pay off the mortgage quickly, using the lender's prepayment privileges to increase your payments or make lump-sum payments will have the same effect as starting with a shorter amortization, without limiting your flexibility.

ARREARS (DEFAULT)

When a borrower is behind in payment obligations, the loan is said to be in arrears. In some cases, the borrower may be described as in default.

If you miss your mortgage payments, usually by the third month a mortgage lender will issue a final demand notice through their solicitor. This will note the amount owing including any additional legal costs or fees incurred. A deadline will be provided for the borrower to make payment, and if this deadline is not met, foreclosure proceedings will begin.

ASSUMABLE MORTGAGE

An assumable mortgage is a type of financing arrangement in which the outstanding mortgage and its terms can be transferred from the current owner to a buyer.

This is a product option that would be desirable if rates started to increase and a buyer might be more enticed to purchase a property if they could also assume a lower interest rate from the seller for the mortgage they would need to purchase the home.

B LENDER (ALTERNATIVE LENDER)

These lenders offer a variety of mortgage products aimed at clients who may be missing income verification or a strong credit history, or who may have been through a consumer proposal or bankruptcy.

B lenders usually require a down payment of 15% or greater. Their interest rates are typically 1% to 3% higher than A lender market rates, with upfront fees of 1% to 3% of the mortgage amount borrowed. Terms offered are usually one to three years.

B lending is ideally a short-term solution to improve a borrower's position so they can convert to an A lender in the future. B lenders like to know the exit plan for the client and how they plan to improve their situation.

B lenders help many families get back on their feet during credit challenges or life events that put them in short-term hardship. B lenders also offer unique options for borrowers that don't necessarily fit into the A lender's boxes at the time.

BANK

A financial institution that accepts deposits from the public and creates credit. Lending activities can be performed either directly or indirectly through capital markets.

Of the top five banks in Canada, two use the broker channel, Scotiabank and TD Canada Trust. The other top banks do not currently lend directly through brokers, but they are usually large investors in monoline lenders within the broker channel. There are many other banks part of the broker channel including, but not limited to: B2B, Bridgewater, CFF, Equitable, ICICI, Manulife and Street Capital.

Banks are regulated by OSFI and the Bank Act, so their products and mortgage specialists do not always have the same guidelines to follow as credit unions and mortgage brokers regulated by FICOM. Bank mortgage officers (sometimes known as mortgage specialists, representatives, advisers or advisors), are not required to complete a mortgage licensing course.

BENCHMARK RATE (AKA QUALIFYING RATE)

The benchmark rate is the posted rate for five-year fixed mortgages published by the Bank of Canada every Thursday. In determining this rate, the Bank of Canada surveys the posted rates of the six major banks and uses the mode (i.e., most commonly occurring rate). All insured borrowers, those with less than a 20% down payment, must now "qualify" at the greater of the contract rate or the benchmark rate as a "stress test" to manage potential future increasing rates. Conventional borrowers as of January 1, 2018, need to qualify at the higher of the benchmark rate or 2% higher than the contract rate.

BONA-FIDE SALES CLAUSE

The borrower is only able to pay off his or her mortgage prior to maturity if the property is sold to a third party.

This is a clause that is more commonly found in mortgage products offering lower-than-usual market rates. This can be a dangerous clause as there is no option to refinance, which could be costly to the homeowner and not worth the initial interest savings the product provided.

BROKER CHANNEL

The two primary ways to arrange a mortgage are to go directly to a bank or credit union or to engage a mortgage broker who represents many lenders and who can advise you and negotiate on your behalf. Not all major banks offer mortgages through mortgage brokers. The "broker channel" refers to those lenders who lend to homeowners, in whole or in part, through brokers.

BROKER NETWORK/SUPER BROKER

The parent company of brokerages and sub-mortgage brokers. There are currently two dominant super brokers in the industry, Dominion Lending Centres and M3 Mortgage Group (owns Multi-Prêts, Mortgage Alliance, Invis, Mortgage Intelligence and Verico). There are a few independent network brokerages including TMG The Mortgage Group, RMA, Axiom, Centum and Broker Financial Group.

BUSINESS DEVELOPMENT MANAGER (BDM) OR BUSINESS RELATIONSHIP MANAGER (BRM)

An employee of a lender who is dedicated to advising mortgage brokers on that lender's product guidelines and policies. They may be the contact that a broker uses to request special file exceptions if an underwriter is not able to do so.

CLOSED MORTGAGE

With a closed mortgage come rates that are lower than the open mortgage alternative. This has made closed mortgages the more popular option in the market. With a closed product there is limited (or possibly no) option to repay the loan early, in full or in part, without prepayment penalties. Prepayment privileges allow smaller lump-sum payments or payment increases without penalty.

CLOSING COSTS

These are costs that can be incurred when purchasing a home, refinancing or switching your mortgage. They include legal fees, transfer fees, disbursements, property transfer tax (PTT) and inspector and appraisal costs. These are in addition to the down payment. Lenders usually request that a borrower prove they have 1.5% of the purchase price available for closing costs, in addition to the down payment. Exceptions can be made for first-time homebuyers, who are not required to pay PTT.

CLOSING DATE

The purchase or refinance date—the day the purchase and sale take place, and/ or the money changes hands. If you have a mortgage, this is the day the loan funds will be released by the lender to complete the purchase or refinance transaction.

Just before or on this day, any outstanding balance of funds from the buyer is due to the solicitor. The lender's funding department issues funds to the solicitor to complete the purchase between buyer and seller. For a refinance, the solicitor will issue any surplus funds to the borrower's account or provide the borrower with a bank draft to deposit.

CO-SIGNER

In cases where an applicant may not be able to be approved for a mortgage due to poor credit score or insufficient income verification, a co-signer can be added to the application. The co-signer will be on the title of the property, but may not be required to live on the property.

COLLATERAL CHARGE

Unlike a standard mortgage, a collateral charge is re-advanceable. That is, once you've paid back a portion of the original loan, or if you haven't taken out the full amount accessible, or the property value has increased, the lender can review and lend additional funds without additional solicitor fees.

Appraisal and qualifying processes are still required, but a collateral charge mortgage could save you the larger fees of a refinance.

The positive aspect of a collateral charge is not having to pay new legal fees if you want to access more equity from your home. The negative, if your mortgage and other debts (say, a line of credit or credit card) are with the same lender and your other debts are not in good standing, those missed payments can be linked to your mortgage account and cause a default on all your borrowing with the bank, including your home mortgage.

Also, if you want to switch lenders later (with no changes to the amount or amortization), you may not be able to without completing a refinance and paying legal fees to re-register the property. In typical switch programs (from mortgage not registered as collateral charges), lenders usually cover the legal fees.

CONTRACT RATE

The interest rate the borrower commits to paying on the mortgage. For monoline lenders, the contract rate is their regular rate.

For banks, the contract rate is usually a rate that is discounted below their "posted" or advertised rates. Bankers may refer to the contract rate as their "discounted rate."

CONVENTIONAL MORTGAGE

The down payment is more than 20% of the value or purchase price. Put another way, these mortgages have a loan-to-value of less than 80%.

With most conventional mortgages (not all), you do not require mortgage default insurance and therefore don't have to pay the premiums a high-ratio borrower (someone with a down payment of less than 20%) is required to pay.

Conventional borrowers may have access to amortizations beyond 25 years.

The recent regulatory changes in the mortgage landscape have put greater emphasis on the LTV as an important part of a borrower's mortgage approval. The percentage of the LTV will influence the interest rate a borrower will pay. Some lenders provide lower rates for borrowers with LTVs 65% or lower.

CREDIT BUREAU

An agency that collects account information from various creditors to create reports on individual borrowing and payment habits. The major credit bureaus in Canada are Equifax Canada and TransUnion Canada.

CREDIT REPORT (CREDIT SCORE OR CREDIT RATING)

A financial report card that creditors use to determine creditworthiness for loan applications. These are generated and accessed through Equifax Canada or TransUnion Canada, who refer to credit reports as credit file disclosures or consumer disclosures, respectively.

Your credit score is one reason it is important to connect with a mortgage broker as soon as you start to think about buying or refinancing. A broker can help you review and, if necessary, improve your score to maximize your borrowing options.

CREDIT UNION

Their products, services and operations resemble those offered by banks, but there are some differences. Specifically, they are made up of a membership; they are locally owned and invest their profits in the communities where they operate and where their members live and work.

Credit unions are regulated by FICOM. With the members as owners, there can be cases where it is more difficult to get an approval, but sometimes they can be more flexible if the client is an existing member. Due to their slightly different regulations and operations, they have unique programs that can sometimes provide more borrowing power or different qualification options.

With most lenders' products, you can port your mortgage to a new home when you move as long as you requalify. This includes inter-provincial moves. With credit unions, porting your mortgage may be restricted to your current area and you may not even be able to port intra-provincially. If your career has a high probability for relocation, a credit union mortgage may not be the best option.

DEBT RESTRUCTURING

See Refinance

DEPOSIT

The amount is selected by the buyer, documented on the contract, and forms part of the purchase price. These funds prove the buyer is serious about the property and completing the purchase. The deposit is usually paid within 24 hours of acceptance (subject removal) and is held *"in trust"* by the buyer's real estate agent until the sale is complete.

DOWN PAYMENT

The amount the buyer is investing towards the purchase price. The source could be personal savings, equity, gifted funds from an immediate family member or, in some cases, non-traditional sources such as borrowed funds.

EQUITY

The portion of the value of a home belonging to a homeowner after the mortgage and any other debts owed on the property are subtracted. As the principal on the mortgage loan is paid, the equity usually increases. Increases in market value and improvements made to the home may add to equity as well.

EQUITY TAKE-OUT (ETO)

An equity take-out mortgage can be accessed through a full refinance, a second mortgage or a home equity line of credit. It provides the borrower with access to the home's equity in cash for common needs such as debt consolidation, investments, down payments and projects such as renovations. Some lenders have a maximum ETO limit.

FICOM

According to the agency's website, the Financial Institutions Commission of British Columbia (FICOM) is the regulatory agency of the British Columbia Government responsible for pension plans, real estate, mortgage brokers, financial institutions (including credit unions, insurance and trust companies) and the Credit Union Deposit Insurance Corporation. For more information, visit: *fic.gov.bc.ca*

If you have concerns or complaints, google FICOM complaints for instructions.

FIRST MORTGAGE

A first lien position on the property title that secures the mortgage. A first mortgage has priority over all other liens or claims on a property in the event of default. In other words, the lender with the first lien receives its money back before any other lenders or liens can receive payment.

FIXED-RATE MORTGAGE

The interest rate stays constant for the term of the mortgage.

Fixed rates give borrowers certainty about their mortgage payment. For the selected term, the borrower knows the interest rate, and therefore the amount of the payments, through to the end of the term.

Prepayment Penalties are usually the higher of the interest rate differential (IRD) calculation or three months' interest.

254

FORECLOSURE

If a borrower defaults on a loan—stops making payments as agreed in the mortgage contract—a lender will proceed with legal action to take possession of the property and sell it to recover their unpaid debt.

FREEHOLD

A type of homeownership. Full and exclusive ownership of property (house and land) for an indefinite period.

FULFILLMENT SPECIALIST

A person who may assist an underwriter in reviewing the documentation (for income, down payment and property) provided by borrowers to meet the conditions of a mortgage commitment.

GROSS DEBT SERVICE RATIO (GDS)

The percentage of the borrower's income that is needed to pay all monthly housing costs (mortgage payments, property taxes, heat and 50% of condo fees or 100% of annual site lease for leasehold tenure). See page 74 for a calculation.

GUARANTOR

In cases where an applicant may not be able to be approved for a mortgage, mostly due to credit score, a guarantor supports the file with his or her credit. The guarantor will not be on the title or be considered an income contributor to the mortgage. A guarantor must usually be a spouse or immediate family member and lenders usually require them to reside on the property.

A guarantor may be the best alternative for an applicant (versus a co-signer) if the applicant wants to meet the qualifications for property transfer tax exemption or the BC HOME Partnership program.

HIGH-RATIO MORTGAGE

The down payment is less than 20% of the value or purchase price. Put another way, these mortgages have a loan-to-value (LTV) higher than 80%.

Mortgage default insurance will be required, with premiums paid by the borrower. Premiums are usually wrapped into the mortgage and amortized with the loan.

Mortgage insurance premiums can be paid up front but are more commonly wrapped into the mortgage and amortized with the loan. Without the option of mortgage default insurance, borrowers would have to save a minimum of 20% of the purchase price.

Especially with housing prices as they are today (particularly in the Lower Mainland and Greater Toronto), mortgage default insurance products help buyers get into the market and start building equity much earlier than they would be able to otherwise.

Somewhat counterintuitively, high-ratio clients are the most desirable in the industry due to the securitization of their loans. The insurance protection gives these borrowers the best rates on the market.

HOME EQUITY LINE OF CREDIT (HELOC)

A HELOC is a line of credit secured by property, so lower rates can be offered compared to a standard, unsecured line of credit.

Unlike a mortgage, the funds don't have to be advanced at closing. Payments are interest-only and are charged only on funds advanced. The interest rate is usually the lender's prime rate plus (+) a premium.

Current regulations limit the HELOC portion of a mortgage to 65% of the property's value.

INTEREST RATE

The rate a borrower pays a lender for the use of its funds. The interest rate and amortization of a loan determine how much the payment will be.

INTEREST RATE DIFFERENTIAL (IRD)

If you pay off your mortgage before your term matures, you will likely have to pay penalties to compensate the lender for the contract breach.

Today, most closed, fixed-rate mortgages have a prepayment penalty that is three months' interest or an interest rate differential (IRD) calculation—whichever is the highest.

Most variable-rate mortgages have only a three-month interest penalty.

The IRD calculation can be drastically different from one lender to another, specifically between a bank and a monoline lender. A good rule of thumb is that an IRD penalty calculation can be 4.5% of the mortgage balance, where three months' interest is approximately 0.5% of the mortgage balance.

For this reason and others, it is important to look at all the aspects of the mortgage product and not just the current rate being offered by the lender for your cost of borrowing.

See page 103 for how IRD can be calculated.

LOAN-TO-VALUE (LTV)

The ratio of a loan amount to the value of the property. *Examples:*

$$\text{High Ratio LTV} \ = \ \frac{\$475,000 \text{ loan amount}}{\$500,000 \text{ purchase price}} \ = \ 95\%$$

$$\text{Conventional LTV} \ = \ \frac{\$400,000 \text{ loan amount}}{\$500,000 \text{ purchase price.}} \ = \ 80\%$$

LEASEHOLD

A type of homeownership. Full and exclusive ownership of property (house and land) for a defined period.

MATURITY DATE

The day the mortgage contract ends. The mortgage can be paid in full, refinanced, renewed or switched to a new lender without penalty on this day.

A refinance can close later than expected and pass the maturity date. Your broker should ensure that your mortgage will convert to an open mortgage so that the refinance can be completed without penalties.

MONOLINE LENDER (MORTGAGE FINANCING COMPANY)

These companies focus solely on mortgages or mortgage-like products secured by real estate. They do not operate storefront locations like the major banks and credit unions. This lowers overhead expenses and the saving can be passed on to borrowers through discounted interest rates.

Monolines also offer unique and flexible mortgage products not available through banks or credit unions and often have lower payout penalties should a borrower break the mortgage contract before maturity.

Although you may not be familiar with monoline lenders' brand names, many have been in the industry for decades and have billions of dollars in residential and commercial financing.

As they don't have storefront locations, they focus on their online and phone customer service presence. For example, First National is repeatedly recognized for its "My Mortgage" client portal, which is one of the most efficient mortgage management systems in the industry. From checking mortgage balances to taking advantage of prepayment privileges, clients can manage one of their most important investments right from their home.

MORTGAGE BROKERAGE

A mortgage company (in some cases a franchise) that manages sub-mortgage brokers to complete mortgage financing.

MORTGAGE COMMITMENT (MORTGAGE APPROVAL)

The mortgage approval from the lender, which outlines the mortgage details and conditions to be met for final approval and funding.

Mortgage commitments vary vastly from lender to lender. There is not one consistent layout required in the industry. All commitments will provide mortgage details (rate, term, amortization and payment) and the conditions. Some will include the prepayment privileges and other lender provisions.

The mortgage commitment is a contract between you and the lender. If something doesn't make sense, ask questions. I also recommend taking a copy of the signed or most recent commitment to the solicitor's appointment to ensure the numbers match. If something is off, contact your broker immediately. The commitment passes through many hands before it arrives to the solicitor and there are many opportunities for human error to occur, especially when it comes to the numbers.

258

MORTGAGE DEFAULT INSURANCE

Allows homebuyers to purchase a home with less than 20% towards the down payment. The borrower pays a premium based on the loan-to-value of the purchase. This can be paid as a lump-sum amount or more commonly included and amortized with the mortgage. The insurance protects the lender should a borrower default on the loan.

MORTGAGE PROFESSIONALS CANADA (MPC)

According to the website, Mortgage Professionals Canada (formerly CAAMP) is Canada's national mortgage broker industry association. In order to help ensure an effective and efficient mortgage marketplace Mortgage Professionals Canada works to:

- Promote consumer awareness of the benefits of dealing with the mortgage broker channel
- Advocate for member interests on legislative and regulatory issues
- Develop, monitor and promote responsible mortgage industry standards and conduct
- Deliver best-in-class training for mortgage professionals
- Provide timely and relevant information to members and mortgage consumers

For more information, visit: *mortgageproscan.ca/en/*

NON-SUBJECT PROPERTY

Property added to the application in addition to the subject property (the one being purchasing, refinanced or renewed). A non-subject property is usually an investment property or a second home owned by the applicant.

This is one of the ways a broker can offer a huge advantage. There are different ways to account for rental property income. The most common, and most conservative, is using

50% of the rental income and adding it back to the borrower's income with 100% of the mortgage payments, property taxes, strata fees and heat accounted for in the borrower's debt service ratios. In the broker channel, there are lenders offering more progressive options for factoring rental income. An "offset" equation or the use of a rental worksheet has the potential to eliminate the negative liability of the rental property or even add a positive cash flow to the application.

OFFICE OF THE SUPERINTENDENT OF FINANCIAL INSTITUTIONS (OSFI)

According to the agency's website, the Office of the Superintendent of Financial Institutions (OSFI) is an independent federal government agency that regulates and supervises more than 400 federally regulated financial institutions and 1,200 pension plans to determine whether they are in sound financial condition and meeting their requirements. For more information, visit: *www.osfi-bsif.gc.ca*

OPEN MORTGAGE

A borrower can pay the mortgage in full or in part, at any time, without penalty.

Lenders charge higher interest rates on open mortgages to compensate them for the costs and risks of possibly having to re-lend the funds in a different interest rate environment. Therefore, open mortgages are the best option only when funds are required for very short terms, such as when you're refinancing and the closing date with the new lender extends past the maturity date of the original mortgage. If your funding needs extend beyond six months, it may be better to consider a variable-rate mortgage with three months' interest penalty costs.

OWNER-OCCUPIED PROPERTY

A property purchased as a principal residence or second home. This can include a home with secondary suites used for rental. This type of purchase can be made with as little as a 5% down payment, whether you are a first-time homebuyer or not.

Mortgages on owner-occupied properties typically have better rates than those on properties purchased for investment purposes. The down payment requirement can be as little as 2.5% in BC if you are a first-time homebuyer taking advantage of the BC HOME Partnership program.

PAYMENT SCHEDULE

Borrowers can select the type of payment schedule they would like for their mortgage. The payment is determined by the mortgage amount, interest rate and the amortization. The payment can be paid monthly, semi-monthly, biweekly, biweekly accelerated, weekly or weekly accelerated. See a breakdown of these options on page 139.

The accelerated payment options allow a borrower to make one additional monthly payment a year, effectively lowering the overall remaining amortization by approximately two to 3.5 years over a five-year term.

PORTABLE MORTGAGE

Portability allows the transfer of a mortgage to another home with little or no penalty when the existing home sells. Mortgage default insurance can also be ported to the new home. Both the mortgage and insurance products will have a restricted time allowable for porting.

To port a mortgage, you must requalify for the mortgage amount you are asking for. Different lender products will have different porting timelines. Most will allow 30 to 90 days to complete a port. Low-frills products usually have restrictive use or no portability options.

POSSESSION DATE

The date the buyer gets possession of the home, receives the keys to the property and is free to move in.

PREPAYMENT PRIVILEGES

Many mortgages feature the ability to make extra lump-sum payments or increased payments without penalty, usually referred to as prepayment privileges.

Lenders commonly offer the flexibility to pay between 10% and 25% (or more) over your regular payments. Some lenders may also offer skip-a-payment, miss-a-payment or double-up payment options. It's important to pay attention to this feature when choosing a mortgage—increasing your monthly payment by a few dollars or using surplus funds as a prepayment can shave time and interest costs off your mortgage.

Some lenders limit prepayments to once a year on the anniversary date, with minimum payments of $1,000. Others allow for lump-sum payments on any payment date with $100 minimums.

Most lenders also offer accelerated biweekly or accelerated weekly payments, which can reduce amortizations by two to 3.5 years over a 5-year term..

PREPAYMENT PENALTY

A fee charged by the lender if more money is paid towards the mortgage than the prepayment options allow. This is commonly owed when a property is sold and the mortgage is being paid out or when the borrower is refinancing mid-term.

PRIME RATE

A lender's prime rate is largely determined by the Bank of Canada's target overnight rate. Historically, the prime rate has been 200 basis points (2%) higher than the target overnight rate. Since 2015, prime has been 2.20% higher than the overnight rate. Refer to the chart on page 98 for changes to the overnight rate since 2006.

PRIVATE LENDER

Private lenders can be individuals or companies known as mortgage investment corporations (MICs). Private lenders are unregulated and therefore do not have to abide by rules set by the provincial or federal governments.

They are mainly interested in the property. The borrower's credit or income may not play a significant role. The lender will review both to get an overall feel for the applicant, but it is the property (location, resale potential and equity) that is important.

Private lenders will consider unique properties as well as offer more flexible options for borrowers requiring construction financing. However, they charge higher interest rates (usually 4% to 10% higher than market rates). They typically want to see a minimum of 35% investment from the borrower.

There are also upfront fees ranging from 2% to 5% of the mortgage amount, but some private lenders charge a higher interest rate with no fees or penalties. Payments are most commonly interest-only with 12-month terms. The lender is hoping to be a short-term solution for the borrower, but usually will have renewal options if payments have been consistent.

PROPERTY TRANSFER TAX (LAND TRANSFER TAX)

A tax charged by many provinces and municipalities that buyers must pay upon closing. Usually a percentage of the purchase price. In BC, the tax is 1% on the first $200,000, 2% on the portion greater than $200,000 up to and including $2,000,000 and 3% on the portion greater than $3,000,000. This tax can be exempt for first-time homebuyers purchasing a property under $500,000 or all buyers purchasing new builds under $750,000.

Other provinces have their own land transfer tax guidelines, while Alberta and Saskatchewan have smaller land title transfer fees.

QUALIFYING RATE (STRESS TEST)

The rate used to qualify the mortgage amount to ensure buyers can continue to afford their homes even if interest rates rise.

High-ratio buyers must qualify at the higher of the benchmark or contract rate. Conventional buyers, as of 2018, will have to qualify at the higher of the benchmark rate or 2% higher than the contract rate.

At the time of writing this book, credit unions have less stringent qualifying requirements for their variable and conventional mortgage rates.

REFINANCE (ALSO REFERRED TO AS A DEBT RESTRUCTURING)

A mortgage process to access equity from one's property. The most common reasons for a refinance are to: take advantage of better interest rates and products, consolidate debts at a lower interest rate, complete renovations or purchase additional real estate.

RENEWAL

During the final 60 to 180 days of your mortgage term, most lenders will contact you with an early renewal offer. By signing the letter, you are accepting the offer and the mortgage will be renewed with your current lender for another term.

It's best to review renewal options with your mortgage broker. At renewal, many banks offer posted rates (non-discounted rates) that are higher than market rates. These can be as much as 2% higher! At renewal, it is also a good time to consider refinance options since penalty costs will not be incurred.

RENTAL PROPERTY

A property that is purchased or currently used as an investment property. This type of purchase requires a minimum of 20% for the down payment, with many lenders requiring a minimum of 25%.

263

Expect to see a 0.25%+ increase in mortgage rates for properties purchased or refinanced as a rental. In the industry, an increase to the rate is known as a bonus and is charged on files that have higher risk or higher cost to the lender.

REVERSE MORTGAGE

A reverse mortgage is a loan secured against the value of your home. Unlike a loan or a regular mortgage, with a reverse mortgage you are not required to make payments. You only repay the loan when you move or sell your home.

This is a specialty product designed mainly for retired or retiring people. It's an option to consider if income levels are too low to service a standard mortgage and there is considerable equity in the property. This gives seniors the option to live at home, without having to feel forced to move and leave their community or downgrade their lifestyle. The interest rates on reverse mortgages are higher than those on standard mortgages.

SECOND & THIRD MORTGAGE

A lien on a property which is positioned behind the first mortgage. Due to the subordinate position, second and third mortgages are riskier, so they can come with higher interest rates and are typically offered for shorter terms.

SOLICITOR

An advisor, lawyer or notary who completes the legal requirements of the mortgage.

STRATA PROPERTY

A type of homeownership. Owners own the unit they live in while they also share ownership of common areas such as the parkade, hallways, elevators, lobbies, gyms, amenity rooms and landscaping with other owners in the building or complex.

264 SUB-MORTGAGE BROKER

An individual mortgage broker, like me. While I'm an independent business owner, being associated with a brokerage allows me to effectively and efficiently process mortgage applications.

SUBJECT PROPERTY

The property being purchased, refinanced or renewed.

SUBJECT REMOVAL DATE

Except in the most competitive of markets, purchase offers are usually made subject to certain conditions, such as the satisfactory completion of a home inspection and financing arrangements. The potential buyer has until the subject removal date to remove these conditions. If financing is not arranged by this date, for example, the seller may agree to extend the date or may choose to "void" the offer in order to accept an offer from another potential buyer.

For a buyer to remove the financing subject, the lender must approve the income, down payment and property documents on or before the subject removal date.

SWITCH/TRANSFER

At renewal, it may make sense to change lenders, either for a better rate or a better product. A switch/transfer program allows a borrower to move the current mortgage "as is" (same amount and amortization) to a new lender. The lender will usually cover legal and discharge fees as an extra incentive to move.

TARGET OVERNIGHT RATE (POLICY INTEREST RATE)

As described on the Bank of Canada's website, the bank carries out the aims of its monetary policy in part by influencing short-term interest rates by raising and lowering the target for the overnight rate. The overnight rate is the interest rate at which major financial institutions borrow and lend one-day ("overnight") funds among themselves; the bank sets a target level for that rate. This target is often referred to as the bank's policy interest rate.

Changes in the overnight rate influence other interest rates, such as consumer loans, mortgages and interest paid on deposits. They can also affect the exchange rate of the Canadian dollar. In November 2000, the bank introduced a system of eight fixed dates each year on which it announces rates. For more information about the target for the overnight rate, refer to the backgrounder on the Bank of Canada's website by *googling: BOC Policy interest rate*.

Changes in the overnight rate usually lead to moves in the prime rate of banks and other lenders. Keeping the rate low encourages borrowing and stimulates the economy. A higher rate increases the cost of credit, lowering demand.

265

TERM
The length of time the mortgage contract is in place. Terms can be open or closed and are usually for six months up to 10 years for fixed, and three and five years for variable.

TITLE
A document giving the named subject legal ownership of a property.

When you receive your title document from your solicitor, review it in detail to ensure the correct names and mortgage charges are registered.

TITLE INSURANCE
Protects what may happen in the future, such as title fraud, and it protects for things that may have happened before the purchase, such as pre-existing work orders or zoning violations. There are two broad types of title insurance, lender and homeowner policies. Most lenders require title insurance to complete a mortgage, which is at the cost of the borrower. The borrower is also responsible for the homeowner policy if they wish to purchase.

TOTAL DEBT SERVICE RATIO (TDS)
The percentage of a borrower's income that is needed to cover housing costs (GDS) plus any other monthly obligations, such as credit card and car payments. See page 74 for a calculation.

UBC SAUDER SCHOOL OF BUSINESS, MORTGAGE BROKERAGE IN BRITISH COLUMBIA COURSE

According to the school's website, the Mortgage Brokerage in British Columbia course is the only course specifically designed to satisfy the minimum educational requirements to become registered with the Financial Institutions Commission (FICOM) Registrar of Mortgage Brokers as sub-mortgage broker in British Columbia.

If you're curious about the course required to be licensed as a mortgage broker, *google: UBC Mortgage Broker*.

UNDERWRITER

The person who reviews and approves (or rejects) mortgage and other loan applications. The underwriter may also be responsible for reviewing all the documentation provided, to verify the applicant's details. He or she is the gatekeeper for the lender and aims to approve only the files that meet the lender's guidelines.

If more documentation is requested, this is the person requesting it. It may be needed to fulfil compliance or other requirements from the lender's guidelines, the insurer and the regulators.

Underwriters may have privileges to give special exception on a file, if needed.

VARIABLE-RATE MORTGAGE

"Variable" is the common term used for floating-interest-rate products. A lender's variable rate is based on its prime rate minus (–) a discount or plus (+) a premium.

There are two variable mortgage products, adjustable-rate mortgages (ARM) and variable-interest-rate mortgages (VRM or VIRM).

Adjustable-Rate Mortgage (ARM)

A mortgage where the interest rate and the monthly payments vary based on changes in market rates. Adjustments to the payment are made if the lender's prime rate changes. The amortization remains the same throughout the term.

Variable-Rate Mortgage (VRM or VIRM)

A mortgage for which the interest rate fluctuates with market rates. The payments will remain the same if there is movement in the lender's prime rate. The amortization period will adjust—longer or shorter—accordingly.

ARM and VRM products give borrowers the option to "lock in"—move from a floating (variable) rate to a fixed rate at any time, without penalty—when the new term is equal to or longer than the term remaining on the original mortgage.

Historically, adjustable/variable-rate mortgages have outperformed fixed-rate mortgages over time, saving borrowers thousands in interest costs.

Penalties are usually limited to three months of interest, and there is no interest rate differential (IRD) calculation.

VENDOR TAKE-BACK MORTGAGE

The seller (vendor) finances the loan for the buyer.

INDEX

268

270

LENDER CONTACTS

Listed below are some of our more popular lenders and their customer service contact details, hours of operation and client portal links.

B2B BANK
Toll-free: 1.800.263.8348
Email: Support@b2bbank.com
Email: Questions@b2bbank.com

BLUESHORE FINANCIAL
Monday to Friday 8:00am to 8:00pm; Saturday 9:00am to 5:00pm (PST)
Phone: 604.982.8000
Toll-free: 1.888.713.6728

BRIDGEWATER BANK
Monday to Friday 7:00am to 5:00pm (MST)
Phone: 1.866.243.4301
Email: customer.experience@bridgewaterbank.ca

CANADIANA FINANCIAL
Monday to Friday 8:00am to 8:00pm (EST)
Toll-free: 1.877.315.1633
Email: cfcmortgagesupport@paradigmquest.com

CANADIAN FIRST FINANCIAL (CFF) BANK
Monday to Friday 9:00am to 6:00pm (EST)
Phone: 1.855.170.3630
Email: customercare@hometrust.ca

CWB OPTIMUM MORTGAGE
Phone: 1.866.441.3775
Email: customer.service@cwbank.com

CMLS FINANCIAL LTD.
Toll-free: 1.888.995.2657
Email: service@cmls.ca
Portal: *https://compassdirect.cmls.ca*

COAST CAPITAL

Monday to Saturday 8:00am to 8:00p; Sunday 9:00am to 5:30pm (PST)

Toll-free: 1.888.517.7000

Metro Vancouver: 604.517.7000

Greater Victoria: 250.483.7000

COMMUNITY SAVINGS CREDIT UNION

Phone: 604.654.2000

Toll-free: 1.888.963.2000

ENVISION FINANCIAL CREDIT UNION

Toll-free: 1.888.221.0027

EQUITABLE BANK

Toll-free: 1.888.334.3313

Email: customerservice@eqbank.ca

FIRST NATIONAL

Monday to Friday 8:30am to 8:00pm (EST)

Phone: 888.488.0794

Fax: 866.325.2563

Email: customer@firstnational.ca

Portal: *www.firstnational.ca/mymortgage*

G&F FINANCIAL GROUP

Monday to Friday 8:00am to 8:00 pm; Saturday 8:00am to 4:00pm (PST)

Sunday and Statutory Holidays: Closed

Phone: 604.419.8888

Toll-free: 1.866.736.GFFG(4334)

HOMEQUITY BANK

Phone: 1.866.331.2447

Email: clientrelations@homequitybank.ca

ICICI BANK

Monday to Friday 8:00am to 8:00pm (local time)

Toll-free: 1.866.726.0825 (English)

Toll-free: 1.866.726.0827 (French)

Email: icicibankmortgagecare@lenderservices.ca

Portal: *www.icicibank.ca/personalbanking/popup-mortgage-login-mob.page?*

LIFECYCLE MORTGAGE

Phone: 1.855.293.7272

Email: vericolcm@paradigmquest.com

MANULIFE BANK

Monday to Friday 8:00am to 8:00pm (across all time zones);

Saturday 9:00am to 5:00pm (EST)

Client Support: 1.877.765.2265

Mandarin Customer Support: 1.888.226.6411

Cantonese Customer Support: 1.888.226.6406

Website: *www.manulifebanmortgages.ca*

Portal: *https://repsourcepublic.manulife.com/wps/portal/Repsource*

MCAP

Monday to Friday 8:00am to 7:00pm (PST)

Toll-free: 1.800.265.2624 (English)

Toll-free: 1.888.811.2529 (French)

Email: service@mcap.com

Portal: *www.mcap.com/residential-mortgages/customers/customer-service*

MERIX

Monday to Friday 8:00am to 8:00pm (EST & PST)

Toll-free: 1.877.637.4914

Email: customerservice@merixfinancial.com

Portal: *https://mymerixhome.merixfinancial.com/Account/LogOn?Retur-nUrl=%2f*

PROSPERA CREDIT UNION

Toll-free: 1.888.440.4480

Website: *www.prospera.ca*

RADIUS FINANCIAL

Toll-free: 1.866.550.8227

Email: radius@lenderservices.ca

Portal: *www.radiusfinancial.ca/site/Customerportal*

RMG
Monday to Friday 8:00am to 8:00pm (EST)
Toll-free: 866.809.5800
Email: MortgageSupport@RMGmortgages.ca
Portal: *https://rmg.entrez.ca/?contact=ad*

SHINHAN BANK CANADA
Phone: 778.284.2640
Website: *www.shinhan.ca*

STREET CAPITAL BANK
Please call or email the contact information under the number representing the first digit in your mortgage number:
"4"
Toll-free: 1.866.939.5005
Email: customer@streetcapital.net
"6"
Toll-free: 1.877.776.6888
Email: support@streetcapital.ca
"7"
Toll-free: 1.866.280.5190
Email: streetcapital@lenderservices.ca
Portal: *https://streetcapital.ca/mystreetmortgage*

SCOTIABANK
Toll-free: 1.800.4SCOTIA (1.800.472.6842)

TD CANADA TRUST
TD Easyline: 1.866.222.3456

WESTMINSTER SAVINGS CREDIT UNION
Phone: 604.517.0100
Toll-free: 1.877.506.0100

XMC MORTGAGE CORPORATION
Toll-free: 1.877.775.2970
Website: *www.xceedmortgage.com*
Portal: *https://xmc.entrez.ca*

ACKNOWLEDGEMENTS

I'm lucky. I am surrounded and supported by strong, encouraging and loving women. If it weren't for my mom, my sister and my aunt, this book may have never come to be. I appreciate all that you do for me, my kids and our family. No words exist to describe the appreciation I have for each of you and for what you give to me. I love you, dearly, and thank you.

Thank you, too, to:

My editor, Lori Bamber: you transformed my dishevelled mom-brain words into a refined and sculpted manuscript that captures my honest, common-sense approach, as you said. Editing was no small feat with this project! Thank you for your patience, understanding, expertise and creativity. You are a master at your art and I can't thank Megan enough for connecting us.

Megan Williams, my publishing coach: thank you for stepping me through this process, much like I step clients through a mortgage. You guided me to options and products I never knew were possible or obtainable. I felt light-years ahead starting with you and your team. In particular, thank you Jazmin Welch and Trista Capitano for your brilliant designs. Inside and out, cover to cover, you made this book on mortgages a work of art.

My husband, Mark, for letting me share our story. You are patient and understanding with my wild and crazy ideas. Although we may not always agree, we find compromise and share complementing characteristics that have a way of elevating us individually and as a family. I hope this book is something we can both be proud of.

To those in the industry, from my brokerages to the lenders, insurers and other veteran and up-and-coming mortgage brokers, you have given me many moments of reflection and heightened my determination to be better and to be one of the best. To a special broker that encouraged me to convert my idea into a book, thank you. Your nudge made the momentum happen.

278 To my clients: if it weren't for you and your continued support, my business wouldn't be compounding as it has. Your trust, honesty and willingness to learn inspired me to write and encourages me to continue to grow and perfect my expertise and customer care. I hope the information in this book helps you fulfill your dreams, and I look forward to supporting you on that sometimes challenging, but always rewarding path.

ABOUT THE AUTHOR

Irene Strong was born in Nakusp, BC, a small village in the West Kootenay region along the Upper Arrow Lakes. It's home to one of Irene's favourite beaches—and pizza subs (from Cutrite Meats). The family moved to Revelstoke, where Irene lived for 10 years before moving to Calgary, Alberta, to complete a joint degree in kinesiology and business management, majoring in marketing, at the University of Calgary.

She has since worked with NBC Olympics Inc., TED Conferences Inc. and Habitat for Humanity Greater Vancouver, among many other organizations. These great organizations have all influenced Irene's mortgage business model, a model built on a foundation of perseverance, education and belief in the power of homeownership.

Being a mortgage broker is a career that comes with great challenges, which have fortunately been far outnumbered by the great successes—assisting her clients in realizing their dreams of owning a home.

Irene now lives in Delta with her husband, Mark, son, Jack, and daughter, Mackenzie. When she is not working on a mortgage file, she is attending events and the kids' activities, playing golf, spending time with friends or working on the next big project. She thoroughly enjoys her time volunteering with Mom2Mom Poverty Initiative Society, a community-based organization focused on improving developmental outcomes for children living in Vancouver's inner city.

IRENE STRONG

STRONGMORTGAGE **PROMISE**

My commitment to you is so strong I felt I had to give it a name. The *StrongMortgage Promise* is a commitment to providing the advice and support, resources, and planning tools required to help you make a confident mortgage decision. To do this, I consider your short- and long-term financial goals as well as the current mortgage market dynamics. My process also includes annual reviews so that you can continue to make the most of your investment today and for all the tomorrows to come.

It's a promise that I'll help you get the mortgage that's right for you, whether that mortgage is completed by my team or not.

Education is the root of the services I provide. In addition to staying current with industry and mortgage product trends, I monitor local and international market and economic indicators that may have an impact on my clients, passing on the information you need to know.

Throughout the year, one of the ways I stay in touch is through my blogs and newsletters. Unlike many similar publications out there, every word is personally written. These are my thoughts, and feelings, whether it's on mortgage topics, sharing my interviews with local realtors, or talking about random interests in the *Me, Myself, and Irene* segment.

The *StrongMortgage Promise* and everything it stands for is designed to help you minimize and manage the stress associated with buying a home or refinancing, providing the expertise you need to make decisions that will serve you and your family in the years ahead.

Made in the USA
Middletown, DE
17 January 2019